Program for the
International Organization of
Social Sciences and Behavioral Research

Fall 2015
November 13-14, 2015

Lynn University/Boca Marriot
Boca Raton, Florida

Conference Program*

*The conference proceedings will be published on amazon.com and the IOSSBR website by December 1st, 2015.

Sponsors and Supporters

IOSSBR would like to thank the following companies and organizations for sponsoring the Fall 2015 Conference:

Academy of Business Research

Amazon.com

Cabells Publishing (www.cabells.com)

Coldwell Banker

European Financial Management Association

Journal of Social Sciences Research

Sentina Publishing

Silver Wheaton

Social Science Resource Network

Conference Staff

Conference Chair

Randall Valentine, Ph.D.

Conference Co-Chair

Robert Reich, Ph.D.

Support Staff

Neelam Kumar Dhungel

Brennan Ladner

Ruth Reich

Dawn Valentine, Ph.D.

Meredith Wilson

Conference Social Activities

Registration: 9:00-4:00 Daily

Snyder Lab - International Business Building (IBC)

Conference Special Presentations

5:30 PM Friday Poster Session

Tap 42, Marriott Town Center

IOSSBR Awards Luncheon

Saturday 12:30 PM

Brio Tuscan Grille, Marriott Town Center

(Included in Registration)

Journal of Social Sciences Research

Complimentary Edition of JSSR
is included in this program

Upcoming Conferences

October 13-14, 2014: Las Vegas, NV
November 3-4, 2014: San Antonio, TX

The *Journal of Social Sciences Research* is published semi-annually. Completed papers accepted to the IOSSBR conference are eligible to be published in the journal. Otherwise, direct submissions may be made to info@iossbr.com.

The journal is a double blind refereed publication. The journal is available in both online and print editions. The journal is open to all topics in social sciences. The journal is listed in Cabells and has a 20% Acceptance Rate.

www.iossbr.com

Journal of
Social Sciences Research

2014 Volume I
Dr. Zack Jourdan, Edi

IOSSBR
Future Conference Dates

<u>Spring 2016 Meeting</u>

Atlantic City, NJ

March 9-11

<u>www.iossbr.com</u>

IBC 213

Behavioral Sciences

Session Chair: Deborah Schadler, Gwynedd Mercy University

**Incorporating Experiential Knowledge of the Elderly in a
Developmental Psychology Class**
Eva Goldhammer, Queensbouough Community College

The Effects of Marital Status on Tipping Behavior
Cameron Moore, University of Southern Mississippi
Stacie Skaggs, University of Southern Mississippi
Tabitha Jordan, University of Southern Mississippi
Aaron White, University of Southern Mississippi
Alexandra Utley, University of Southern Mississippi
Elizabeth Borrow, University of Southern Mississippi
Dominique Lynn, University of Southern Mississippi
Michael Mong, University of Southern Mississippi

**Vocational Rehabilitation Services and Outcomes for Transition-Age Youth with
Traumatic Brain Injuries**
Phillip Rumrill, Kent State University
Richard Roessler, Independent Rehabilitation Consultant, Fayetteville, Arkansas
Fong Chan, University of Wisconsin
Malachy Bishop, University of Kentucky

A Model for Community Collaboration by a Small University: The Autism Institute
Deborah Schadler, Gwynedd Mercy University
Catherine Heller, Gwynedd Mercy University

10:00 AM Friday November 13th

IBC 214

Social Sciences

Session Chair:

Breast Cancer- A Worldwide Health Problem: Meaning, Coping, Social Support and Health of Women with Early Stage Breast Cancer
Kathleen Sternas, Seton Hall University

***Tips from Former Smokers* Campaign on a University Campus**
Melinda Ickes, University of Kentucky
Karen Butler, University of Kentucky
Mary Kay Rayens, University of Kentucky
Amanda Wiggins, University of Kentucky
Melody Noland, University of Kentucky
Ellen Hahn, University of Kentucky

Cross-Disciplinary Infusion of Quantitative Reasoning (QR) in College Courses
Janet Michello, LaGuardia Community College

Self Care for the Aging - We Are All Aging
Veronika Ospina-Kammerer, Saint Leo University
Christine Gordon, Saint Leo University

10:00 AM Friday November 13th

IBC 308

Social Sciences

Session Chair: Tracy Nichols, Austin Peay State University

**Service Learning and Social Media:
Examination from a Local and Global Perspective**
Emily DeSpain, Austin Peay State University
Julia Batson, Austin Peay State University

**Communication in Organizations:
An Exploration of Local and Global Experiences**
Amber Botts, Austin Peay State University

**An Analysis of Greater Tennessee's Sexual Health Education with
Special Focus on Consent Education**
Keedy Burdeshaw, Austin Peay State University

**Hip and Flipped: Engaging Students in General Education to
Upper Division Courses via High Impact Practices Coupled With the
Flipped Classroom Concept**
Tracy Nichols, Austin Peay State University

IBC 314

Education

Session Chair: Sanne Unger, Lynn University

From Abstract to Concrete: The Challenge to Redefine the Way Undergraduates Interpret and Present the Peer Reviewed Journal Article
Keturah Mazo, Florida Institute of Technology

Inspiring Online Learning Success for our Under Represented Student Populations
Mary-Lynn Chambers, Allied American University

Multiliteracy in the 21st Century Classroom: It's Time to Get Creative!
Mary-Lynn Chambers,   Elizabeth City State University

Maximizing Benefits of Hybrid Courses
Sanne Unger, Lynn University
Carrie Simpson, Lynn University
Shara Goudreau, Lynn University
Darren Allen, Lynn University

Session Chair:

**A Four-Stage Prediction Model for Job Satisfaction for
Employed Adults with Multiple Sclerosis**
Jian Li, Kent State University
Richard Roessler, Independent Rehabilitation Consultant, Fayetteville, Arkansas
Phillip Rumrill, Kent State University

**High-Priority Employment Concerns of Hispanics/Latinos with
Multiple Sclerosis in the United States**
Phillip Rumrill, Kent State University
Richard Roessler, Independent Rehabilitation Consultant, Fayetteville, Arkansas
Jian Li, Kent State University
Karla Anhalt, Kent State University
Malachy Bishop, University of Kentucky

Lessons from Tbilisi, Georgia
James Decker, California State University Northridge
Jodi Brown, California State University Northridge
Christina Bame, California State University Northridge
Jessica Tapia, California State University Northridge

Investigating Memory Deficits in Aging Adults
Gina Glanc, Texas A&M University Corpus Christi
Jesica Logan, Rice University

1:00 PM Friday November 13th

IBC 214

Social Sciences

Session Chair:

Technology Based Education: A Foe or Friend to Student Development?
Harika Rao, Lynn University

Solving the Unemployment Paradox
Harika Rao, Lynn University

Constructing the Truth:
An Examination of Economic Opportunity Costs for Sports Facility Funding
Brent C. Estes, Sam Houston State University
Ryan K. Zapalac, Sam Houston State University

Session Chair:

**Soap Operafication: A Content Analysis of the Evolution of a
Genre and Devolution of Reality**
Tracy Nichols, Austin Peay State University
Mike Dunn, Austin Peay State University

Zen Gardens
Kenneth Lee, CSUN

The Consumer (r)Evolution:
From Rational and Irrational Behavior, to Programmatic Consumption Behavior
Matteo Peroni, Lynn University
Michele Peroni, Lynn University

**Conversion as a Professional Success Strategy Among the 19th Century
European Jewish Musical Elite: The Case of Ignaz Moscheles**
Marsha Dubrow, The Graduate Center, CUNY

IBC 314

Education

Session Chair: Ramakrishnan Menon, Georgia Gwinnett College

Virtual Field Experiences: Teacher Candidate Opinions
Duane Giannangelo, University of Memphis

Zero Tolerance: Useful or Useless
William Rieck, University of Louisiana at Lafayette

**Preparing White Preservice Principals for Leading
Non-White Student Populations**
Mack Hines, Sam Houston State University

An Analysis of Desegregation Cases under the Obama Administration
Joe Dryden, Texas Wesleyan

Exposing Fallacies, And Scams Resulting from Mathematical Ignorance
Ramakrishnan Menon, Georgia Gwinnett College

Session Chair:

Health Care Priorities and Preferences of Americans with Multiple Sclerosis
Malachy Bishop, University of Kentucky
Michael Frain, Florida Atlantic University
Timothy Tansey, University of Wisconsin-Madison
Phillip Rumrill, Kent State University
Brad McDaniels, University of Kentucky

**Anticipated Versus Unanticipated Monetary and Fiscal Policies
Under Rational Expectations**
Dawit Senbet, University of Northern Colorado

The Myth of "Right-Turn Bias" in Public Places
Stephen Bitgood, Jacksonville State University

**Does Confucianism Give an Excuse to Korean Mothers for
Using Psychological Control?**
Sun-A Lee, University of Louisiana, Lafayette
Charles Allen Lynn, University of Louisiana, Lafayette

5:50 PM Friday November 13th

Tap 42, Marriott Town Center

Poster Session

Differential Neural Activity of Low and Highly Hypnotizable Individuals While Experiencing Moderately Painful Stimuli
Mattie N. Crockett, University of Virginia's College at Wise
Kristina Feeser, University of Virginia's College at Wise
James W. Stowers, University of Virginia's College at Wise
James E. Horton, University of Virginia's College at Wise
Dennis McClain-Furmanski, University of Virginia's College at Wise

Hidden Voices: L2 Students' Compensatory Writing Strategies
Nancy Stockall, Sam Houston State University
Corinna Villar Cole, Sam Houston State University

Mississippi Gulf Coast Social Bias on Marriage Equality: A Lost Letter Experiment
Stacie Skaggs, University of Southern Mississippi
Tabitha Jordan, University of Southern Mississippi
Cameron Moore, University of Southern Mississippi
Elizabeth Borrow, University of Southern Mississippi
Alexandra Utley, University of Southern Mississippi
Aaron White, University of Southern Mississippi
Michael Mong, University of Southern Mississippi

10:00 AM Saturday March 14th

IBC 213

Behavioral Sciences/Social Sciences

Session Chair: Deniz Yucel, William Patterson University of New Jersey

Young Children's Development within the Context of Place: An Examination of the Contribution of the Physical Environment (Skype)
Elizabeth Matthews, City College, City University of New York

Deciding Factors in a Stay-at-Home Father and Working Mother Relationship
Cassie Russing, Amberton University
Misty Sparks, Texas Wesleyan University

Prospects of Developing a Psychological Theory of Experience as an Alternative to Kantian
Amir Salehi, Community College of Baltimore County

Psychopathology of Leadership
Lani Fraizer, Pepperdine University
Farzin Madjidi, Pepperdine University
Gabriella Miramontes, Pepperdine University

Exploring Partnership Brokering and its Potential in Social Change Making
Lani Fraizer, Pepperdine University and Yunus Center at Asian Institute of Technology
Faiz Shah, Yunus Center at Asian Institute of Technology
Farzin Madjidi, Pepperdine University

Parent-Child Relationship Quality and Peer Bullying among Early Adolescents: The Mediating Effect of Internalizing Problem Behavior and the Moderating Effect of Gender
Deniz Yucel, William Patterson University of New Jersey

10:00 AM Saturday March 14th

IBC 214

Social Sciences

Session Chair:

Using Theatre of the Oppressed to Empower Young, Low-Income Parents
Deborah Byrd, Lafayette College

"Sharing Their Art" in Detention: The Effect on Youth and Staff
Jill Leslie Rosenbaum, California State University, Fullerton

Police Officers and Crime:
An Analysis of Crimes Committed by Police Officers in the State of Florida
Steven M. Hougland, Bainbridge State College
Jennifer M. Allen, University of North Georgia

Rate at Which Lesbian, Gay, and Bisexual Citizens Are Victims of
Physical Assaults Due to Their Sexual Orientation
James Jones, Lincoln University

Can Wittgenstein Use Cooley's Looking Glass?
Paul Wilson, Texas State University

10:00 AM Saturday March 14th

IBC 308

Education

Session Chair:

Global Leadership Scores of Entering Doctoral Students
June Schmieder-Ramirez, Pepperdine University

Who's Running the Schools?
Kathleen Campbell, Southeastern Louisiana University
Nan B. Adams, Southeastern Louisiana University

**Examining the Use of Narrative Feedback as the Primary Mode of Assessment:
To What Extent Is Narrative Feedback a Useful Assessment Technique?**
Charles Gleek, Lynn University

1:00 PM Friday November 13th

Brio Tuscan Grille, Marriott Town Center

Awards Luncheon

Name	Affiliation	Page
Adams, Nan B.	Southeastern Louisiana University	19
Allen, Darren	Lynn University	10
Allen, Jennifer M.	University of North Georgia	18
Anhalt, Karla	Kent State University	11
Bame, Christina	California State University Northridge	11
Batson, Julia	Austin Peay State University	9
Bishop, Malachy	Kent State University	7,11,15
Bitgood, Stephen	Jackson State University	15
Borrow, Elizabeth	University of Southern Mississippi	7, 16
Botts, Amber	Austin Peay State University	9
Brown, Jodi	California State University Northridge	11
Burdeshaw, Keedy	Austin Peay State University	9
Butler, Karen	University of Kentucky	8
Byrd, Deborah	Lafayette College	18
Campbell, Kathleen	Southeastern Louisiana University	19
Chambers, Mary-Lynn	Allied American University	10
Chan, Fong	Kent State University	7
Cole, Corinna Villar	Sam Houston State University	16
Crockett, Mattie N.	University of Virginia's College at Wise	16
Decker, James	California State University Northridge	11
DeSpain, Emily	Austin Peay State University	9
Dryden, Joe	Texas Wesleyan	14
Dubrow, Marsha	The Graduate Center, CUNY	13
Dunn, Mike	Austin Peay State University	13
Estes, Brent C.	Sam Houston State University	12
Frain, Michael	Florida Atlantic University	15
Fraizer, Lani	Pepperdine University and Yunus Center at Asian Institute of Technology	17
Freeser, Kristina	University of Virginia's College at Wise	16
Giannangelo, Duane	University of Memphis	14
Glanc, Gina	Texas A&M University Corpus Christi	11
Gleek, Charles	Lynn University	19
Goldhammer, Eva	Queensbouough Community College	7
Gordon, Christine	Saint Leo University	8
Goureau, Shara	Lynn University	10
Hahn, Ellen	University of Kentucky	8
Heller, Catherine	Gwynedd Mercy University	7
Hines, Mack	Sam Houston State University	14

Horton, James E.	University of Virginia's College at Wise	16
Hougland, Steven M.	Bainbridge State College	18
Ickes, Melinda	University of Kentucky	8
Jones, James	Lincoln University	18
Jordan, Tabitha	University of Southern Mississippi	7, 16
Lee, Kenneth	California State University, Northridge	13
Lee, Sun-A	University of Louisiana, Lafayette	15
Li, Jian	Kent State University	11
Logan, Jessica	Rice University	11
Lynn, Charles Allen	University of Louisiana, Lafayette	15
Lynn, Dominique	University of Southern Mississippi	7
Madjidi, Farzin	Pepperdine University	17
Matthews, Elizabeth	City College, City University of New York	17
Mazo, Keturah	Florida Institute of Technology	10
McClain-Furmanski, Dennis	University of Virginia's College at Wise	16
McDonald, Brad	University of Kentucky	15
Menon, Ramakrishnan	Georgia Gwinnett College	14
Michello, Janet	LaGuardia Community College	8
Miramontes, Gabriella	Pepperdine University	17
Mong, Michael	University of Southern Mississippi	7, 16
Moore, Cameron	University of Southern Mississippi	7, 16
Nichols, Tracy	Austin Peay State University	9, 13
Noland, Melody	University of Kentucky	8
Ospina-Kammerer, Veronika	Saint Leo University	8
Peroni, Matteo	Lynn University	13
Peroni, Michele	Lynn University	13
Rao, Harika	Lynn University	12
Rayens, Mary Kay	University of Kentucky	8
Rieck, William	University of Louisiana, Lafayette	14
Roessler, Richard	Independent Rehabilitation Consultant, Fayetteville, AR	7,11
Rosenbaum, Jill Leslie	California State University, Fullerton	18
Rumrill, Phillip	Kent State University	7,11,15
Russing, Cassie	Amberton University	17
Salehi, Amir	Community College of Baltimore County	17
Schadler, Deborah	Gwynedd Mercy University	7
Schmieder-Ramirez, June	Pepperdine University	19
Senbet, Dawit	University of Northern Colorado	15
Shah, Faiz	Yunus Center at Asian Institute of Technology	17
Simpson, Carrie	Lynn University	10

Skaggs, Stacie	University of Southern Mississippi	7, 16
Sparks, Misty	Texas Wesleyan University	17
Sternas, Kathleen	Seton Hall University	8
Stockall, Nancy	Sam Houston State University	16
Stowers, James W.	University of Virginia's College at Wise	16
Tansey, Timothy	University of Wisconsin-Madison	15
Tapia, Jessica	California State University Northridge	11
Unger, Sanne	Lynn University	10
Utley, Alexandra	University of Southern Mississippi	7, 16
White, Aaron	University of Southern Mississippi	7, 16
Wiggins, Amanda	University of Kentucky	8
Wilson, Paul	Texas State University	18
Yucel, Deniz	William Patterson University of New Jersey	17
Zapalac, Ryan K.	Sam Houston State University	12

Countries Represented at 2014-2015 IOSSBR Conferences

Canada
Denmark
India
Iran
Kuwait
Nepal
Netherlands
Pakistan
South Korea
Switzerland
Romania
Turkey
United Kingdom
United States
Vietnam

www.iossbr.com

Journal of

Social Sciences Research

2014 Volume I
Dr. Zack Joordan, Editor

Volume I

2015

The Journal of Social Sciences Research is a publication to support research of all topics in social sciences. Manuscripts with subject areas submitted to the journal include, but are not limited to, anthropology archaeology, communication, criminal justice, economics, education, geography, health care, history, interdisciplinary studies, international relations, linguistics, political science, psychology, sociology, women's studies, and other related areas of research.

The Journal of Social Sciences Research is published semi-annually by the International Organization for Social Sciences and Behavioral Research (IOSSBR). The journal is a double blind referred publication and is listed in Cabells with a 20% acceptance rate.

All articles should follow APA format and be submitted via MS Word format to: info@iossbr.com.

IOSSBR 2015 Conference Location

Fall 2015

November 13-14

Lynn University

Boca Raton, Florida

www.iossbr.com

Table of Contents

Using Undergraduate Learning Assistants to Enhance Student Retention and Academic Success

Sarah M. Stout
Bowie State University

Katrina S. Kardiasmenos
Bowie State University

Cheryl Blackman
Bowie State University

ABSTRACT

During the 2011-2012 Academic Year, the Department of Psychology redesigned the General Psychology course (PSYC 101) with the aim of enhancing the quality of course instruction, improving student success and reducing administrative costs. As part of the redesign, Undergraduate Learning Assistants (ULAs) who were upper-level psychology students with demonstrated academic success, served as peer mentors/tutors for the PSYC 101 course. These ULAs tutored PSYC 101 students who experienced difficulty with course content, provided feedback on assignments, and acted as liaisons between the students, graduate assistants, and the PSYC 101 instructors. Results indicated that students were more likely to meet with ULAs than with the instructors, and those students who met with the ULAs were more likely to earn an A, B, or C in the course as compared to those who did not meet with them. Furthermore, results indicated that the number of times a student met the ULAs for assistance directly contributed to the overall score earned by the student in the course. Further exploration of the impact of peer tutoring and mentoring on academic success is warranted.

Introduction

Over the past 10 years advances have been made in teaching undergraduate psychology courses (Brewer, 2006). The earlier methods of teaching which included lecturing to students and then testing them on what they had learned, have been shown to be less effective with today's generation of students (Barnes, Marateo, & Ferris, 2007; Junginger, 2008; Machese, 2006; Malm, Bryngfors, & Morner, 2011; McGlynn, 2008; Stewart, 2009; Wilson, 2008). Supplemental Instruction (SI) has emerged as a teaching method that assists students by increasing their academic success and reducing their withdrawal rates. Dr. Deanna Martin introduced SI in 1974 at the University of Missouri – Kansas City with the intention of increasing that institution's retention rates (Martin & Arendale, 1992). Since then, many institutions have introduced various forms of SI into their high-risk (that is, courses with a failure rate greater than 30%) introductory courses and have seen promising results (Congos & Schoeps, 1993).

Researchers have discovered that one of the most prominent elements of SI is peer tutoring. Carter and McNeill (1998) defined a peer tutor as one student that gives educational support to another student, but maintains a higher academic classification. The results from previous studies have been mixed. In some instances, researchers have not found peer tutoring to be beneficial to a student's academic success (Carter & McNeill, 1998; Malm, Bryngfors, & Morner, 2011; McDonnell, Mathot-Buckner, Thorson, & Fister, 2001; McDuffie, Mastropieri, & Scruggs, 2009; Smith, 2008) although research has observed an improvement in other student characteristics. For example, recently, Malm et al. (2011) found that students who received assistance from peer tutors in their program were more open to accepting help from classmates. Other studies reported that tutees have become less competitive (McDonnell et al., 2001). This suggests that students are less disruptive and aggressive towards other students after receiving help from peer tutors (McDonnell et al., 2001). Furthermore, students provided positive feedback regarding their peer tutoring experiences (McDuffie et al., 2009) and even students that did not receive peer tutoring reported an appreciation that it was available if needed (Smith, 2008).

Alternatively, other research has demonstrated an increase in student success as a result of peer tutoring (Burns, 2006; Dioso-Henson, 2012; Cooper, 2010; McDonnell et al., 2001; Ning, & Downing, 2010). For example, McDonnell et al. (2001) found that students, both with and without disabilities, benefitted academically from peer tutoring. Burns (2006) found that tutees improved their ability to self-correct after a peer tutor provided continual praise. Arco-Tirado, Fernandez-Martin, and Fernandez-Balboa, (2011) and Dioso-Henson (2012) discovered that students who received peer tutoring had improved knowledge and greater retention of course content than students who did not receive any type of tutoring. Interestingly, Carter and McNeill (1998) found that students might need less assistance from tutors at the end of a course as compared to the beginning.

In addition to the academic benefits that may result from receiving peer tutoring, students reported other benefits. For example, Baron (1997) found that students reported having a higher self-image because of the similarity they saw between themselves and their peer tutors. Dennett and Azar (2011) demonstrated that tutees felt that peer tutors were easier to relate to than their instructors, making them more likely to seek assistance from their peers. Vogel, Fresko, and Wertheim (2007) reported that tutees and tutors found the tutoring relationship more beneficial when they shared a similar educational background. In addition, tutees believed that the tutors explained the material in a manner that was easier to understand than when it was presented by an instructor (Flyr, 2000).

Previous research has found an impact of peer tutoring on student success, but it has mostly been examined at the institutional level (Arco-Tirado et al., 2011; Baron, 1997; Carter & McNeill, 1998; Cooper, 2010; Quinn, 1991). The impact of peer tutoring on student success at the level of the course has also been examined, but the results have been mixed (Burns, 2006; Dioso-Henson, 2012; McDonnell et al., 2001). Cooper (2010) found that the number of times a student met with peer tutors had a positive impact on student success. However, the impact had a greater effect in the semester following the peer tutoring experiences when overall GPA was the dependent measure. This line of research has not examined the number of times a student met with a peer tutor for assistance and whether that could be used to predict the student's overall grade in the class.

The purpose of the current research was to examine the impact of peer tutoring in an introductory-level course, specifically, General Psychology (PSYC 101) at Bowie State University, a regional comprehensive university, and the oldest historically black university in Maryland. PSYC 101 is a gateway course for all psychology majors and a general education course required by most majors at the University. As such, the course serves 200-250 students per semester. In previous years, PSYC 101 yielded a DFW rate (that is, the number or students who earned a final grade of D, F, or who withdrew from the course) of 38% making it a "high risk" course, with a DFW rate greater than 30% (Congos & Schoeps, 1993).

In order to enhance academic success at the university, the Department of Psychology redesigned PSYC 101 beginning Fall 2011 in an effort to increase student retention and decrease the number of students who have to repeat the course. As part of the redesign, the department incorporated Undergraduate Learning Assistants (ULAs), who served as peer tutors/mentors for students enrolled in the course. The role of a ULA was to tutor PSYC 101 students who experienced difficulty with course content, provide feedback on assignments, and act as a liaison between the students, graduate assistants, and PSYC 101 instructors. All ULAs must participate in an initial training session the week before classes begin. They also receive ongoing training throughout the semester. During the initial training, and throughout the semester, they learn about best practices in peer tutoring, effective communication with students, providing constructive feedback to students, and how to deal effectively with cultural and personality differences. With training, ULAs learn to identify when it is necessary to refer a student to an instructor or other resources offered by the university.

Therefore, based on previous research findings, it is hypothesized that: (1) A higher percentage of students who sought help from peer tutors will be successful in the course as compared to those who did not seek help from peer tutors, (2) The frequency of peer tutor/tutee contact would be positively related to the grade earned in the course, and (3) Students will be more likely to seek help from peer tutors as compared to the instructors.

Method

Participants

Students in PSYC 101. A total of 244 undergraduate students (Female = 173, Male = 71) were enrolled in the PSYC 101 course, among 5 sections, at the beginning of the Fall 2012 semester. Over the duration of the first week of class, students were informed that their performance in the course might be used as part of a larger research study on the effectiveness of different teaching methods in PSYC 101. Students were asked to provide written consent if they were willing to have their performance included as part of this research study. Therefore, this study reports the results of data for the 218 undergraduate students (Female = 155, Male = 63), with an average age of 19.96 (M = 19.96, SD = 3.04, $range$ = 17-41) who signed the consent form. Table 1 includes demographic and academic information for these 218 students.

Table 1

Demographic information for students enrolled in PSYC 101 during the Fall 2012 semester

	N	%
Total Number of Students	218	100%
Gender		
Male	63	28.9%
Female	155	71.1%
Race		
African American	200	91.7%
Hispanic	7	3.2%
Caucasian	2	0.9%
Asian	3	1.4%
2 or More Races Specified	5	2.3%
Native Hawaiian	1	0.5%
Year in School		
Freshman	135	61.9%
Sophomore	55	25.2%
Junior	13	6.0%
Senior	14	6.4%
Not Specified	1	0.5%

Undergraduate Learning Assistants (ULAs). A total of seven undergraduate (Female = 4, Male = 3), upper-level psychology majors, with an average age of 25.14 years ($M = 25.14$, $SD = 4.95$, $range$ = 20-34) served as ULAs during the Fall 2012 semester. At the beginning of the semester, ULAs were informed that their interactions with the PSYC 101 students might be examined to determine the importance of their role. All ULAs provided written informed consent. Table 2 includes demographic information for the ULAs.

Table 2

Demographic information for ULAs during the Fall 2012 semester

	N	%
Total Number of ULAs	7	100%
Gender		
Male	3	42.86%
Female	4	57.14%
Race		
African American	7	100%
Year in School		
Junior	3	42.86%
Senior	4	57.14%

PSYC 101 Instructors. A total of four PSYC 101 instructors (Female = 4), with doctoral degrees taught PSYC 101 in the Fall 2012 semester. Two instructors were Caucasian, one was African American, and one was bi-racial. With the exception of the bi-racial instructor who taught two sections of PSYC 101 during the Fall 2012 semester, the other instructors only taught one section each. The instructors' teaching experience varied from 4 years to 10 years.

Design

The PSYC 101 course sections used a common syllabus and common assignments. All students enrolled in PSYC 101 had the opportunity to seek help from the ULAs, but could make the choice regarding whether they did so or not.

Materials

The materials for the research included the assignments that were part of the PSYC 101 curriculum. The curriculum of PSYC 101 was centered on Laura E. King's *Experience Psychology* (1st ed.) published by McGraw-Hill. Students enrolled in the PSYC 101 course attended two 50-minute lectures and one 50-minute lab per week. In lab, students completed chapter quizzes and small-group activities with their classmates. Students completed four exams over the course of the semester as well as three writing assignments. After being given step-by-step instructions on how to find a research article on the library databases, students were instructed to write an outline of the first experiment of the article, based on a set of guidelines provided by the instructor. The second writing assignment required students to write a summary of the second experiment of the article, based on the sample outline. The third writing assignment required students to show a deeper understanding of the course content by choosing concepts that had been covered in class, and reflecting on how those concepts could be applied to their own lives. Students also had to complete an anonymous survey designed specifically to find out how many times they had received assistance from the instructor, graduate assistants, or ULAs, and whether those meetings were helpful or not. Sign-in sheets were used to document student contacts with the ULAs. Information included the student's name, the date and time, and the type of assistance needed (e.g., make-up quiz, help with writing assignments, help with course content, etc.).

Procedure

On the first day of classes, students were given the syllabus for the course, introduced to the graduate assistants and ULAs, and the instructor reviewed the syllabus. The instructor also verbally informed the students that their performance in the class might be used to assess the efficacy of the course redesign.

During their first lab, students received the informed consent form. It was stated that they were not required to sign the consent form, and would not be penalized for not signing it. All PSYC 101 students had the same requirements for completing the course, but only data for those who provided consent were included in this study.

Over the course of the semester, whenever students visited with a ULA, they were asked to sign in and to indicate the reason for their visit. All email correspondence from students requesting assistance was collected and tabulated. During the last lab session of the semester, students were given a paper-and-pencil version of the "End-of-Semester Survey." Students were informed that their responses would be anonymous.

Grades from all five sections of the PSYC 101 course were calculated using a prescribed formula based on points earned. The frequency of face-to-face contacts between ULAs and students was tallied along with contact made via emails. Therefore, each student could be classified as having sought help or not. Survey data were recorded and analyzed separately.

Results

Of the 244 students enrolled in the PSYC 101 class during the Fall 2012 semester, 218 of them signed consent forms. Only the data from those 218 students were included in the analyses. An initial analysis of student grades as a function of race of instructor did not yield significant results, $F(2, 137) = 2.153$, n.s. Therefore, the data were collapsed across all sections.

Hypothesis I

A chi-square was calculated to determine if students who asked for assistance from the ULAs were more likely to pass the class (that is, earned an A, B, or C) than those students who did not ask for assistance from the ULAs. As shown in Figure 1, results of the chi-square determined that there was a significant relationship between asking for assistance from the ULAs and passing the course, $\chi^2(1) = 10.49$, $p = .001$, $\phi = .2$. Specifically, of the 107 students who received assistance from the ULAs, 88.8% passed the course, while only 71.2% of the 111 students who did not receive assistance from the ULAs passed the course.

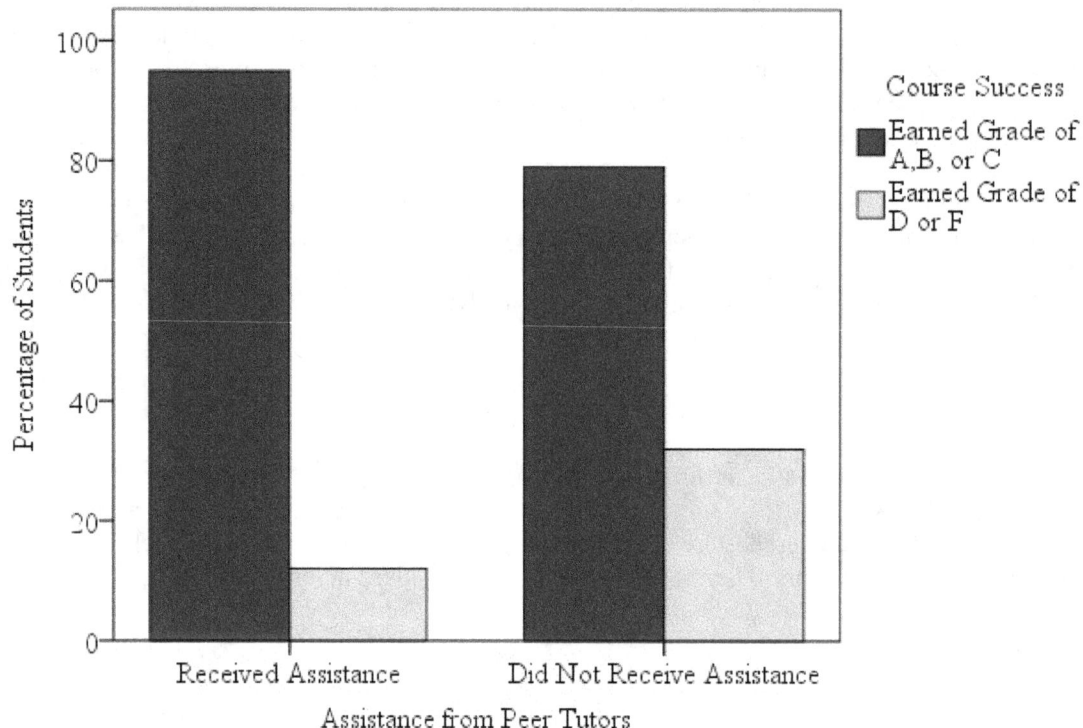

Figure 1. The percentage of students who passed or failed the course as a function of whether they received assistance from the peer tutors. This figure indicates that a higher percentage of students passed if they received assistance.

Hypothesis II

To determine whether the number of visits to the ULAs for assistance could predict overall percentage earned in the class, a regression analysis was calculated. The results of the regression indicated that the number of times students received help from the ULAs accounted for 5.1% of the variance in the final percentage earned in the class.[1] For each time help was sought from ULAs, the final percentage in the class increased by 3.3 percentage points, $F(1, 209) = 11.32, p = .001$.

---

[1] To determine if additional factors accounted for a greater amount of variance in the final percentage earned in the class, a multiple regression was conducted using the total number of times students received help, overall SAT scores, and the GPA students had upon entering the University. The University assigns a GPA of 0.00 to first-semester students, including freshmen and transfer students. This 0.00 is not a true measure of students' academic ability, and so they would have to be excluded from the analysis. However, exclusion would account for 36.2% of the students, and the results would only be generalizable to students who had earned a GPA at the University (that is, continuing students). Therefore, to make the results more generalizable, entering GPA was included. None of the additional factors were reliable predictors of percentage earned in the class, and the number of times a student asked for help was no longer significant, $p > .05$. This is not a surprising finding given that the inclusion of additional factors decreased the power of the model.

Hypothesis III

A paired-samples t-test analyzed whom students reported seeking assistance from more: the instructor or the ULAs. As shown in Figure 2, the paired-sample t-test indicated that students sought assistance from the ULAs ($M = 1.08$, $SD = 1.778$) significantly more than they did from the instructors ($M = 0.80$, $SD = 1.425$), $t(180) = -2.126$, $p = .035$. The effect size for this analysis ($d = 0.158$) was small according to Cohen's (1988) conventions.

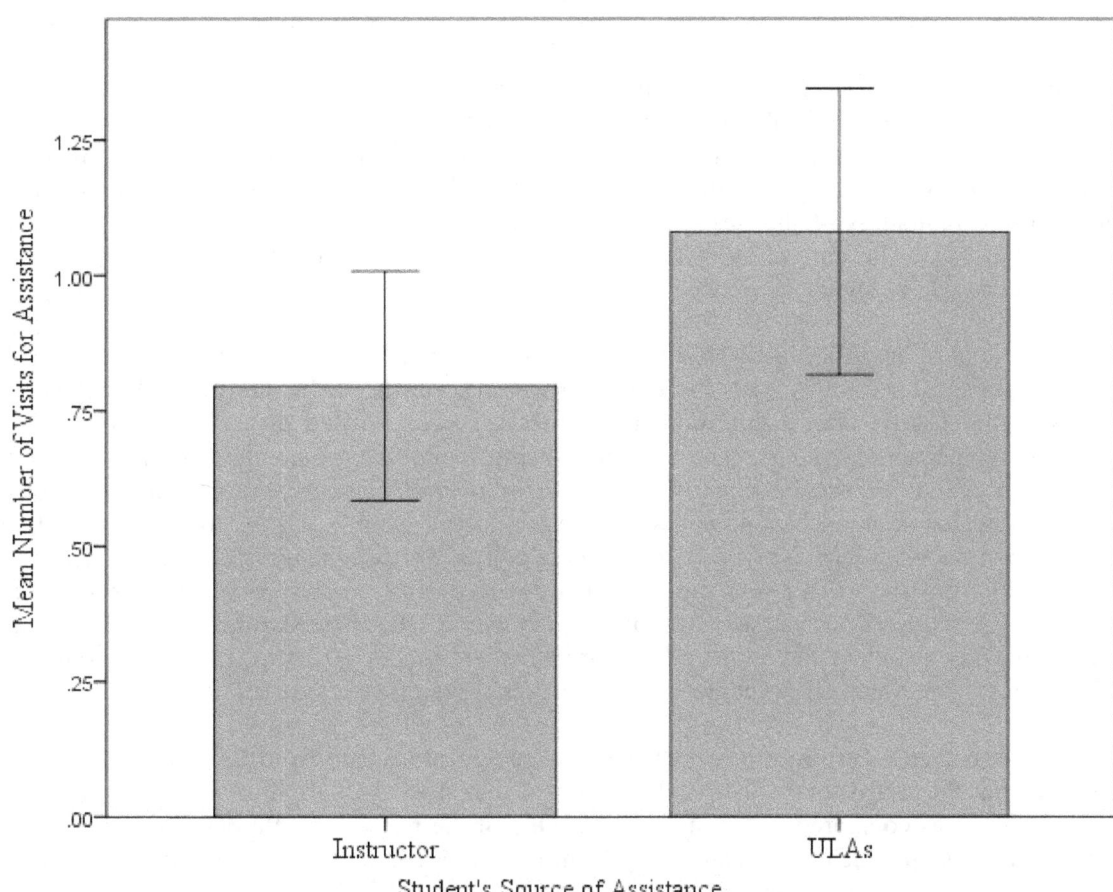

Figure 2. The mean number of visits to the instructor or ULAs for assistance. This figure indicates that the students visited the ULAs more than the instructor during the Fall 2012 semester.

Discussion

The current study examined whether students who received help from the ULAs would be more likely to pass the course compared to those who did not receive help from the ULAs. Additionally, the research examined if there was a specific impact on a student's grade earned in the course in relation to the number of times a student met with peer tutors. Lastly, the current study examined if students would be more inclined to seek help from the ULAs over instructors.

For Hypothesis I, there was a higher percentage of success recorded for students who had received assistance from the ULAs when compared to students who did not receive assistance from the ULAs. This is consistent with other research that has shown academic success for individual courses (Burns, 2006; Dioso-Henson, 2012; McDonnell et al., 2001). Other studies have been unable to find a significant effect of peer tutoring on academic success (Arco-Tirado et al., 2011; Carter & McNeill, 1998; Evans, Flower, & Holton, 2001; Malm et al., 2011; McDonnell et al., 2001; McDuffie et al., 2009; Smith, 2008; Solomon & Crowe, 2001), which may have been due to the presence of limiting factors. These factors were not present in the current study. For example, Evans et al. only offered peer tutoring during class time. The researchers reported that the tutors and the tutees found this arrangement extremely difficult because the tutors were addressing the entire class rather than giving individual attention as is the case in the current study. Other researchers neglected to thoroughly train their tutors (Solomon & Crowe, 2001). The current study utilized 7 tutors, which enabled the researchers to limit confounds brought on by inexperienced tutors.

While previous research has measured positive effects of peer tutoring on various measures of academic success, this study took these findings a step further. Distinctively, Hypothesis II addressed the specific effects the number of times a student visited the ULA had on overall earned course percentage points. The current research found that the number of times a student met with a peer tutor can be directly predictive of overall percentage points in the course. Results indicated that each time assistance was sought from a ULA, the student's final percentage in the class increased by 3.3 percentage points. In fact, the number of times a student sought help from the ULAs was more predictive of overall earned course percentage than entering GPA and SAT scores (see Footnote 1). Cooper (2010) also examined the impact of the number of times a student met with a peer tutor on student success. However, Cooper's outcome variable was institutional GPA and not performance in a specific course.

The third hypothesis examined whether students sought assistance from the ULAs more than they did from the instructors. The results indicated that students were more likely to seek help from the ULAs as compared to the instructors. One of the reasons for this finding may be that students are less apprehensive seeking help from a peer as compared to an instructor (Carter & McNeill, 1998). Another explanation may be that the ULAs make the content more understandable than the instructors (Flyr, 2000) and are perceived as being easier to relate to by students (Dennett & Azar, 2011).

In most peer tutoring programs, the tutors are volunteers and are neither paid nor recruited for the positions, because of budgeting constraints. However, some researchers explain that most tutors volunteer because of various personality traits which are rooted within the tutor. Some notable traits that have been continually reported are trustworthiness and having a strong sense of responsibility (Daddona, 2011; Dennett & Azar, 2011; Evans et al., 2011). Logically following those findings, research also suggests that tutors are more inclined to want to help others (Daddona, 2011). Additionally, Gines (2000) found that tutors were smarter, had a higher maturity level, and were more cooperative than the average student. Despite these traits that provide the potential for students to volunteer to be tutors, research indicates that to have a successful peer tutoring program, thorough training is imperative (Cervantes, Lieberman, Magnesio, & Wood, 2013). In the current study, although training is conducted to provide the PSYC 101 students with the best possible peer tutoring experience, it may not be as extensive as proposed by previous research (Parkinson, 2009; Smith, 2008; Wilson & Arendale, 2011).

Furthermore, research has described how peer tutoring specifically benefitted first-year students. The first year of college is an important time of transition for students, and peer tutors have been found to have a positive impact on academic success during that time (Weinsheimer, 1998). Rae and Baillie (2000) examined third-year tutors assisting first-year students, and found that the tutoring experience gave the first-year students a pleasant introduction to college life. Nearly 62% of the students enrolled in PSYC 101 at the university are considered first-year students, or freshmen. While the current study found an overall positive effect of peer tutoring on academic success in the course, it did not specifically examine this impact in the first-year students. It also did not examine any effects on tutees' personal feelings about the experience. In future research, it would be worthwhile to examine these effects more thoroughly.

Supplemental instruction, specifically peer tutoring, is growing in popularity at many educational institutions. Building upon the findings from previous research, the current research has provided evidence that when executed appropriately, peer tutoring can be a cost-effective and successful means of improving a student's academic success. Furthermore, the specific impact on a student's academic success in a particular course can be predicted based on the number of times a student seeks help from a peer tutor. Further research should include other factors such as training and personality characteristics of tutors when examining the specific impact on a student's academic success and the reasons why students seek assistance more from a peer tutor.

At most universities, students have to go to tutoring centers to receive assistance. Having tutors embedded in the classroom is a non-traditional and effective way of utilizing peer tutors. Vincent Tinto, from Syracuse University, and widely hailed as a specialist in student success, retention, and persistence at the college level, suggests three linked sets of activities and support that will promote student education. Specifically, he first suggests that programs should contextualize academic support. This refers to the practice of linking developmental education and study skills to courses in which these skills will be used. Second, he suggests that programs employ collaborative and cooperative pedagogies that allow students to learn together. He explains that students are more successful when they are academically and socially engaged. Finally, Tinto suggests that programs should connect classroom activities to campus student support services. This tutoring and mentoring approach brings support to students and faculty as well as leadership opportunities to participating tutors.

References

Allen, T. D., Eby, L. T., & Lentz, E. (2006). Mentorship behaviors and mentorship quality associated with formal mentoring programs: Closing the gap between research and practice. *Journal of Applied Psychology, 91*(3), 567-578.

Arco-Tirado, J., Fernandez-Martin, F., & Fernandez-Balboa, J. (2011). The impact of a peer-tutoring program on quality standards in higher education. *Higher Education: The International Journal of Higher Education and Educational Planning, 62*(6), 773-788.

Barnes, K., Marateo, R., & Ferris, S. (2007). Teaching and learning with the net generation. *Innovate: Journal of Online Education 3(A),* 1 -8.

Baron, W., (1997). *The problem of student retention: The Bronx Community College solution--the freshman year initiative program.* New York, NY: Bronx Community College.

Brewer, C. L. (2006). Undergraduate education in psychology: United States. *International Journal of Psychology, 41*(1), 65-71.

Burns, E. (2006). Pause, prompt and praise--peer tutored reading for pupils with learning difficulties. *British Journal of Special Education, 33*(2), 62-67.

Carter, K., & McNeill, J. (1998). Coping with the darkness of transition: Students as the leading lights of guidance at induction to higher education. *British Journal of Guidance and Counseling, 26*(3), 399-415.

Cervantes, C. M., Lieberman, L.J., Magnesio, B., & Wood, J. (2013). Peer tutoring: Meeting the demands of inclusion in physical education today. *The Journal of Physical Education, Recreation & Dance, 84*(3), 43-48.

Cohen, J. (1988). *Statistical Power Analysis for the Behavioral Sciences* (2nd Edition). New Jersey: Lawrence Erlbaum.

Congos, D. H., & Schoeps, N. (1993). Does supplemental instruction really work and what is it anyway? *Studies in Higher Education, 18*(2), 165-178.

Cooper, E. (2010). Tutoring center effectiveness: The effect of drop-in tutoring. *Journal of College Reading and Learning, 40*(2), 21-34.

Curators of the University of Missouri. (n.d.). *The International Center for Supplemental Instruction: Deanna C. Martin, Ph.D.* Retrieved from http://www.umkc.edu/asm/si/martin.shtml.

Daddona, M. F. (2011). Peer educators responding to students with mental health issues. *New Directions for Student Services,* (133), 29-39.

Dennett, C. G., & Azar, J. A. (2011). Peer educators in a theoretical context: Emerging adults. *New Directions for Student Services,* (133), 7-16.

Dioso-Henson, L. (2012). The effect of reciprocal peer tutoring and non-reciprocal peer tutoring on the performance of students in college physics. *Research in Education, 87*(1), 34-49.

Evans, W., Flower, J., & Holton, D. (2001). Peer tutoring in first-year undergraduate mathematics. *International Journal of Mathematical Education in Science & Technology, 32*(2), 161-173.

Flyr, M. (2000). Assistance center helps students make the grade in Nebraska. *Community College Week, 12*(24), 23.

Gines, A. C. (2006). Teaching undergraduate psychology in the Philippines: A summary of current programs, policies, and instruction. *International Journal of Psychology, 41*(1), 51-57.

Junginger, C. (2008). Who is training whom? The effect of the millennial generation. *FBI Law Enforcement Bulletin, (77),* 19-23.

Kardiasmenos, K.S., Blackman, C., Lynch, A.M., Haynes, M., & Wagoner, T. (2013). Improving student learning and success through the use of course redesign techniques. *Journal of Social Sciences Research, March,* 70-79.

Malm, J., Bryngfors, L., & Morner, L. (2011). Supplemental instruction: Whom does it serve? *International Journal of Teaching and Learning in Higher Education, 23*(3), 282-291.

Martin, D. C., & Arendale, D. R. (1992). Supplemental instruction: Improving first-year student success in high-risk courses. *The Freshman Year Experience: Monograph Series No. 7.* Columbia, SC: National Resource Center for the Freshman Year Experience, University of South Carolina.

McDonnell, J., Mathot-Buckner, C., Thorson, N., & Fister, S. (2001). Supporting the inclusion of students with moderate and severe disabilities in junior high school general education classes: The effects of class wide peer tutoring, multi-element curriculum, and accommodations. *Education and Treatment of Children, 24*(2), 141-160.

McGlynn, A. (2008). Millennials in college: How do we motivate them? *Education Digest, (73)6,* 19-22.

McDuffie, K. A., Mastropieri, M. A., & Scruggs, T. E. (2009). Differential effects of peer tutoring in co-taught and non-co-taught classes: Results for content learning and student-teacher interactions. *Exceptional Children, 75*(4), 493-510.

Ning, H. K., & Downing, K. (2010). The impact of supplemental instruction on learning competence and academic performance. *Studies in Higher Education, 35*(8), 921-939.

Parkinson, M. (2009). The effect of peer assisted learning support (PALS) on performance in mathematics and chemistry. *Innovations in Education & Teaching International, 46*(4), 381-392.

Quinn, T. (1991). The influences of school policies and practices on dropout rates. *NASSP Bulletin, 75*(538), 73-83.

Rae, J., & Baillie, A. (2005). Peer tutoring and the study of psychology: Tutoring experience as a learning method. *Psychology Teaching Review, 11*(1), 53-63.

Smith, T. (2008). Integrating undergraduate peer mentors into liberal arts courses: A pilot study. *Innovative Higher Education, 33*(1), 49-63.

Solomon, P., & Crowe, J. (2001). Perceptions of student peer tutors in a problem-based learning programme. *Medical Teacher, 23*(2), 181-186.

Stewart, K. (2009). Lessons from teaching millenials. *College Teaching, 57(2).* 111-118

Twigg, C. A. (1999). *Improving learning and reducing costs: Redesigning large-enrollment courses.* Troy, NY: Center for Academic Transformation Rensselaer Polytechnic Institute.

Vogel, G., Fresko, B., & Wertheim, C. (2007). Peer tutoring for college students with learning disabilities: Perceptions of tutors and tutees. *Journal of Learning Disabilities, 40*(6), 485-493.

Weinsheimer, J. (1998). Providing *effective tutorial services.* Washington, DC: National Council of Education Opportunity Associations.

Wilson, J. (2008). The millennials: Getting to know our current generation of students. *International Journal of Scholarship of Teaching and Learning, 5*(1), 1-12.

Wilson, W. L., & Arendale, D. R. (2011). Peer educators in learning assistance programs: Best practices for new programs. *New Directions for Student Services,* (133), 41-53.

Acknowledgements

This study was supported by a grant awarded to Katrina S. Kardiasmenos, Ph.D., by the University System of Maryland's Course Redesign Initiative.

We express our gratitude to Brenna Smothers and Morgan Haynes for their assistance with entering data; Gayle Fink from the Office of Planning, Analysis and Accountability for providing entering GPAs and SAT scores. We would like to also express our gratitude to Deborah M. Clawson, Ph.D. and Erica Hernandez, Ph.D. for assistance with the statistical analyses.

Division of Household Labor in Stay at Home Father & Working Mother Families

Cassie Rushing
Amberton University

Misti Sparks
Texas Wesleyan University

Lisa Powell
Amridge University

ABSTRACT

Working mother, stay-at-home father is a family structure that is becoming increasingly more common, and demands attention. A phenomenological qualitative study was utilized to explore division of household labor within a stay-at-home father and working mother relationship. A total of 20 working mothers were interviewed regarding how they handle household labor within their home as well as contributing factors to this decision. All participants were married, heterosexual women with biological children ages 1 to 4 and who worked outside the home and the father stayed home as primary caretaker and did not contribute financially. Results indicated that the division of household labor was a collaborative process. Participant responses are included, and implications for practice are discussed.

Introduction

Traditional roles within a family are changing as gender roles become more flexible in societal constructs. Women have been seen as caretakers, nurturers and homemakers, but are now in the workforce more than ever. While women are becoming career oriented, men are taking on the caretaking and home making role. According to Heppner and Heppner (as cited in Fischer & Anderson, 2012), men and women are challenging the stereotypical gender roles and are participating in nontraditional roles of employed mothers and caregiving fathers. The number of families where the mothers are employed full-time outside the home and fathers stay home to care for children continues to grow. According to the 2010 Bureau of Labor Statistics (as cited in Fischer & Anderson, 2012), women now make up 47% of the labor force. The 2012 U.S. Census Bureau reported there are 24.4 million married fathers with children younger than 18 (U.S. Census Bureau, 2012a). The Census Bureau also reported that 189,000 identified themselves as stay-at-home fathers in 2012, which was defined as remaining outside the labor force for at least 1 year so they can care for their family while their wife works out- side the home (U.S. Census Bureau, 2012b). It was also identified that these fathers cared for an upward of 369,000 children (U.S. Census Bureau, 2012b). The U.S. Bureau of Labor and Statistics stated that at the start of the 21st century, only a third of U.S. households enact the male breadwinner model and nearly another third have the female as the breadwinner (as cited in Meisenbach, 2010).

Division of Labor

Division of labor is a topic that has been explored for decades and has been a topic of conversation in many relationships. Now that family dynamics are changing, it is important to know if division of household labor is also shifting. More women are entering the workforce, meaning less time at home. Parents in two earner families have the responsibilities of their jobs, household and children (Wood & Repetti, 2004). Due to these multiple roles, many question whether or not labor is divided more equally in a dual earner home. Another drastic change society sees is the growing number of stay-at-home fathers. Others question if fathers staying home with children take on more of the household duties.

Inequality in Division of Labor

Inequality in division of labor has been studied for decades. According to Coltrane women still do most of the housework, despite their increased participation in the workforce (as cited in Poortman & Van Der Lippe, 2009). A couple can perceive equality and inequality in a relationship based on the division of family work. If this is perceived unequal, it could impact a person's psychological well-being (Tao et al., 2010). Women who hold nontraditional values and roles perceive the division of labor as unfair, and perceived unfairness has been related to psychological distress and marital conflict (Eshleman & Bulcroft, 2006). Researchers have also found that when individuals perceive that they are doing more than their fair share of household labor, they experience distress as well as anger and rage (Lively, Steelman, & Powell, 2010; Claffey & Mickelson, 2009). When division of household labor is perceived as fair and equitable, both husband and wife report fewer depressive symptoms (Kalmijn & Monden, 2012).

The study by Lothallar, Mikula, and Schoebi (2009) examined multiple factors that contribute to the imbalance of division of labor between dual earner couples. Some of the factors identified were time availability, gender ideology, and the importance of characteristics of the family system (Lothallar et al., 2009). The study hypothesized that the more time women spent in professional work and the more time men spent at home, the more the division of labor would be balanced based on time availability at home. However, the study showed that this was not the case. Time availability did not balance out division of labor. The division of work was imbalanced to the woman's disadvantage as she still took on more household labor (Lothallar et al., 2009). Additionally, Dunn, Rochlen, and O'Brien (2013) investigated the identity and adjustment experiences of this subset of working mothers and found that one of the disadvantages of working mother stay-at-home father arrangements was that mothers expressed frustrations and disappointments related to the cleanliness of the home or other home care tasks.

The gender ideology model illustrates that people make decisions based on their traditionalism of gender attitudes. According to Lothallar, Mikula & Schoebi (2009), men with less traditional gender attitudes do more family work and women with less traditional gender attitudes do less family work compared to those with more traditional attitudes. They also found that those with nontraditional views were less likely to have less imbalanced division of labor.

Deciding Factors

There are many factors that contribute to the division of labor in couples (Coltrane, 2010). Studies have shown that employed women still take on most of the housework (Eshleman & Bulcroft, 2006). Childhood and family values play a huge part in how household labor is decided. Girls are raised to take pride in their home by cleaning, decorating and nurturing the home. A study by Cunningham showed that parental attitudes towards household duties are predictive as to how children view and participate in division of labor in their own marriages (as cited in Eshleman & Bulcroft, 2006). Poortman and Van Der Lippe (2009) found that women showed a positive attitude towards cleaning, cooking, and child care. Women also showed higher standards and feelings of responsibility regarding household chores.

Working from the supposition of previous researchers (Coltrane, 2000) that even though wives perform approximately twice as much household labor as their husbands, they report fairness in the division of labor, Kawamura and Brown (2010) sought to explore whether or not this is impacted by *mattering*. They defined *mattering* as beliefs about supportiveness, as evidenced by respect, concern, and appreciation. Their findings suggest that the more wives believe they matter to their husbands, the more likely they are to report fairness in division of household labor, regardless of actual time spent engaged in these processes.

Changes to Division of Labor

Gender inequality of the division of household labor is beginning to change to accommodate the flexibility of gender roles. Changes in the division of labor reflect changes in societal views (Eshleman & Bulcroft, 2006). Two-earner families have the ability to have a more balanced division of child care and housekeeping compared to single earner families (Wood & Repetti, 2004). Rehel (2014) found that when fathers are encouraged to take extended leave following the birth of a child, and engage in a dynamic of coparenting, rather than the more traditional helper role, an opportunity for the development of a more gender-equitable division of labor is created.

Methods

A qualitative phenomenological study was utilized to explore division of household labor in stay-at-home father and working mother relationships. "Qualitative research attempts to make sense of or interpret phenomena in terms of the meanings people bring to them" (Denzin & Lincoln, 2013, p. 7). Phenomenology explores the meaning of the lived experiences of several individuals and its purpose is to create a universal meaning to reduce individual experiences (Creswell, 2007). The researcher explored the mother's subjective experience of how household labor is handled among the stay-at-home father and working mother family dynamic. This design allowed the mothers to not only share their perspective but also allowed society to understand these family dynamics from the mother's subjective experience and create a more universal meaning to the stay-at-home father and working mother phenomenon.

The theoretical implications of the study were guided by choice theory. Choice theory explains that we choose everything we do. It explores how and why we make choices that guide our lives

(Glasser, 1998). This theory aided the understanding of how division of household labor is handled, the contributing factors to this decision and how this choice affected their family dynamics.

The research was conducted in accordance to the policies and procedures of the Capella University Institutional Review Board. This board consists of scholars and researchers who work to ensure all procedures are followed to protect participants from harm and informed consents follow protocol to ensure privacy and anonymity (Leedy & Ormrod, 2005). A copy of the institutional review board's approval was then provided to participants to report credibility for the research.

Participants

Participants of the study were twenty working mothers who met sample characteristic criteria. The characteristics of each mother were married, heterosexual women with biological children ages 1 to 4 wherein their husband was the full-time caregiver and she worked full- time outside the home.

The researcher used multiple marketing techniques to reach participants that met the criteria. The sites www. meetup.com and www.athomedad.org were utilized to identify local parenting groups. A search for key words "stay-at-home dads," "working mothers," "stay-at-home parents," and "local playgroups" were used to identify groups specific to the study population. A request for participation was posted on each site to recruit participants. Twenty-one elementary schools in the local area were also contacted and asked to send flyers home to the parents. Seven web forums were contacted and a post was placed on each site requesting participants.

Twenty mothers met the requirements for participation and were recruited for the study. Five participants were from the researcher's home state of Texas, 5 participants were recruited from Missouri, and 10 participants were recruited from Illinois, for a total of 20 participants. No participants chose to withdraw from the study. The majority of participants (95%) identified themselves as Caucasian. Of the 20 participants, 60% of the population reported an income of >110,000. The mothers' education level identified that 90% were college graduates or postgraduate and 75% of the fathers held a college or postgraduate degree. Ninety-five percent of the participants reported this was a first marriage for them and their husbands. Sixty-five percent of the families reported having two children in the home. The mothers' occupation varied with 25% of the participants reporting being attorneys.

Data Collection

The techniques that were used in the qualitative study were interviews and audio recordings. Multiple data collection techniques, such as direct observations, interviews, and documentation are qualitative strategies that enhance data credibility (Baxter & Jack, 2008). This ensured that the issue explored was not examined through one lens but rather a variety of lenses that allows for multiple facets of the phenomenon to be revealed and understood (Baxter & Jack, 2008). The interviews were conducted at a location chosen by the participant. The researcher ensured that the location met requirements regarding privacy and confidentiality of the participant as well as quietness to successfully interview. The researcher took into consideration time and location in an attempt to provide a comfortable environment for the participant.

When the participant and researcher first met face-to- face, the informed consent was reviewed and the purpose of the study and the risks and benefits were thoroughly covered with the participant. Then, the participant signed the informed consent in front of the researcher. Once the signed informed consent was obtained, the researcher collected the demographic questionnaire and qualifications checklist from the participant. These were already filled out by the participant as they were mailed previously in the recruitment packet.

Once the demographic and qualifications checklist was received, the open-ended, unstructured interview questions were asked. The questions were as follows: (1) Describe for me in detail how the division of household labor is handled in your home; (2) Discuss some of the factors that influenced the decision on how the division of household labor was developed. The questions were unrestricted in time to allow the participant to answer fully. Prompts were used as a means to clarify and expand the participant's response.

Data Analysis

All participants were interviewed face to face and these interviews were audio recorded. Qualitative researchers believe interviewing and observation are ways to gain a better picture into the participant's perspective (Denzin & Lincoln, 2013). Tape-recordings were then transcribed by a court reporter employed by the researcher. The researcher asked the participant immediately after the interview if they could be contacted a minimum of 1 month following the interview. The researcher invited each participant to review the written transcripts provided by the transcriptionist following each interview. If permission was given, the participant was contacted by electronic email. The emailed packet provided a transcription of their personal interview. Participants were asked to review and contribute additional material or clarify their statements. Seventeen participants took time to review and send transcription back to researcher and 2 of the 17 chose to make additional comments.

Once interviews were transcribed, the researcher began classification to identify themes in the transcriptions. The researcher and two experts searched for themes. The two experts hold a doctoral degree and have extensive training in qualitative research. When forming themes, the researchers and experts used interpretation. During the process of interpretation, researchers form larger meanings of what is going on in the situations (Creswell, 2007). According to Barritt (as cited in Leedy & Ormrod, 2005), the purpose data analysis is to identify common themes in the personal experiences.

Finally, the transcriptions were uploaded into the qualitative software program NVivo, where the researcher was able to combine and subdivide codes and ultimately form consistent themes throughout the transcripts. Computer-assisted software permitted frequency counts and tabulations (Denzin & Lincoln, 2003). NVivo helped manage and shape unstructured information by using visualization tools such as chart, graphs, and models. NVivo provided security by storing the databases and files together in a single file and enabled the researcher to manipulate the data and conduct searches (Creswell, 2007). Once coding and identification of themes were created, the expert panel and researcher reread the transcripts to ensure accuracy and thoroughness.

Field Testing

A list of the interview questions was prepared and sub- mitted to a panel of experts. The panel consisted of three therapists with extensive training and experience in children and family counseling. All three experts hold a doctoral degree and have a background in qualitative research. They all are licensed therapists in the state of Texas. None of the experts were affiliated with Capella University. The panel analyzed the questions and pro- vided feedback on how to improve the quality of the interview questions. All feedback was taken into consideration and changes were made to the original questions.

Reliability and Validity

Reliability in a qualitative study is concerned with ensuring the study is of quality. According to Gibbs, (as cited in Creswell, 2009) a reliable study identifies that the researcher's findings are consistent across other research studies and projects. Essential criteria for qualitative reliability are credibility, consistency, and applicability. Steps were put in place to monitor reliability in the study.

According to Bronfenbrenner (1976, as cited in Meisenbach, 2010), member checking is an accepted source of validity checking in phenomenological studies (Meisenbach, 2010). In this case, the researcher engaged in an in-depth member checking protocol where each participant was emailed a copy of the transcript and asked for any feedback and clarification. Also, after completing the study, each participant was contacted again and given a full copy of the final study before final submission. Twelve of 20 participants responded to the final submission identifying no concerns and expressing gratitude for the study.

There were steps in the data collection phase that were taken to ensure reliability. All procedures of the research were documented. This includes data collection and analysis techniques. Transcripts from interviews were transcribed and checked against the tape-recording to ensure they do not contain any mistakes. During data analysis, it is crucial to pay specific attention to coding. The researcher made sure there was not a misunderstanding in definition or meaning of codes.

To ensure understanding, data are compared with codes numerous times and crosschecked with the definitions of the codes (Creswell, 2009). These codes were also cross- referenced with codes developed by the expert panel.

Credibility

According to Mertens (2005), credibility tests the correspondence between the way the respondents perceive the questions and respond and the way the researcher portrays their understanding of their responses. Constructivism and triangulation were two strategies the researcher used to ensure the research was credible.

A constructivist paradigm assumes there are multiple realities, the knower and respondent co-create understandings, and procedures are in a natural setting (Denzin & Lincoln, 2003). Constructivism values multiple realities (Golafshani, 2003). Multiple methods of data collection were used to acquire multiple realities. These methods were interviews and audio recordings. Also having 20 participants allowed the researcher to gain 20 different perspectives.

Analyst triangulation was also used to support credibility. Triangulation is when a researcher uses multiple investigators as a way to corroborate evidence from different sources to shed light on a theme (Creswell, 2009). Using multiple methods and data sources will help strengthen interpretations in qualitative study (Mertens, 2005). The strategy to ensure triangulation in the study was having numerous techniques of analyzing the data. The professional transcriptionist transcribed all audio recordings. The transcribed data were then analyzed by the researcher and three experts for themes. Then, the data were uploaded into the qualitative soft- ware NVivo to analyze for themes. Using multiple methods of analyzing data ensured triangulation.

Results

Division of Household Labor Was a Collaborative Process

The significant theme that emerged was that division of household labor was a collaborative process. The participants provided a wide range of responses regarding how household labor is handled in their home. Eighty five percent of the participants identified many aspects to collaboration such as strengths and skill set, personal standards and preferences, supportive spousal relationship, compassion and respect. Due to their ability to work together, the participants shared they felt that household labor was a more collaborative approach. This partnership allowed for their time at home to be more flexible and they were able to spend more time with their family instead of on household chores and duties. The theme of collaboration was expressed in the following quotes:

> I would say from a numbers perspective, he does 90% and I do 10%. If you're looking at it from a subjective perspective then we consider it to be balanced. We look at it like he does what he does for our family and home and I do what I do for our family and home. It's just different roles. – Participant 13

> We've just decided that he would do whatever it takes to keep the house running and I would step in whenever I could and pick up the slack, so on weekends, I help out. You know, so on the weekends, I may throw a little laundry in. I try to cook on weekends, you know, special meals for the family. I do all of the financial stuff - Participant 6

My husband does all the grocery shopping. He basically does all the dishes. We both do laundry. In the summer, he does the yard work. I like to putter in the garden but I don't always have time to do that but in terms of mowing the lawn, he does that and the snow shoveling in the winter. Those are probably the main things. Bills were one of those things that I finally handed over to him because I kept being late getting bills paid and we decided he needed all these online bills to go to him rather than me. Participant 18

A common response of utilizing strengths and skillset was noted by the participants as a way of dividing household labor. Participants acknowledged that they work more effectively as a partnership when they focus on their strengths. This was demonstrated in the following examples:

My husband is just particular about the dishes. He kind of took that on. And I think he would probably say I'm particular about the cleaning so that's why that responsibility kind of falls to me. And I think we really, since the time when we first lived together, I think we had all those fights then and sort of figured out like our thresholds for household chores and that sort of thing. – Participant 9

I think personal preference. There's always this task that you hate doing. And, what we each like to do probably has a lot to do on how we make those decisions. For instance, I like things neat and organized so every night I will do a regular walk through and pick up. – Participant 10

I hate dishes and he's okay with it. So, he does all the dishes. It has just evolved. He has a much lower sense of smell than I do so he is fine with taking out the trash, where the smell bothers me. I care more about the major cleaning, like bathrooms, so I like to do that on the weekends so I know it's done. Participant 14

Personal standards and preferences regarding cleanliness also played a role in the decision of how household labor would be handled. Eight of the participants acknowledged that they choose the responsibility of various household chores due to their own standards of cleanliness. Five of these participants acknowledged hiring a cleaning service to help maintain their level of cleanliness. These participants felt that hiring service to help maintain their level of cleanliness would reduce conflict in their relationships and ensure their personal standards were met. Personal standards and preferences were demonstrated by the following examples:

We do have a housekeeper that comes every week. And every other week she kind of does a full cleaning of the house and then the interval week she does a couple of hours of vacuuming and does the floors in the kitchen and basics like that. But that's been a huge help and that is something we started doing long before we had kids That's a huge relief because I don't have to spend time that I can otherwise be spending with the kids in the weekends or the evening's cleaning. – Participant 10

I do my own laundry because I'm very picky about gentle cycle, what gets dry and what gets hung and whatever. He really never does the bathroom to the detail and extent which I think it should be done or the frequency. So I do the bathrooms – Participant 3

I'm kind of picky about my laundry and so that's one of those things that we get behind on because I have trouble relinquishing-- he always says relinquish, that's his word. He wants me to relinquish control of things and I've gotten better at that during three and a half years. But, we do have a cleaning service that cleans the house every other week. That helps too. – Participant 18

A supportive spousal relationship was also noted as a factor in providing a collaborative approach to division of household labor. Participants acknowledged that when they felt supported in their role as primary breadwinner, they were more likely to work with their partner in completing household chores, if needed. Participants discussed the importance of feeling respected and valued in their role as the working mother. The theme of supportive spousal relationship was displayed in the following quotes:

It goes back to that central tenant that my husband is a believer that his job is to take care of the house and that my job is to work outside of the home. And so, he does the majority of things at home. He does the laundry, the grocery shopping, and the cleaning. He runs all the errands, he cooks, just anything that needs to be done at home, you know, minor repairs, he'll do that. He doesn't view himself as just the caretaker. It's everything that goes with running a household he feels that he should be responsible for. Participant 6

He just volunteers. He really does. He volunteers to do everything, because he knows I've been really stressed over the last couple of years with my mom being sick and my grandmother just got sick and she was in the hospital for a couple of months so after work I'd go home and change and then go straight into the a hospital all night. So for about a month I barely saw my child. So I think he realizes that I just can't handle everything and so he just knows what to pick up and what to do just so I don't have to stress and break down. Because I can't do it all. He is just the best husband in the world. – Participant 2

It's like our rules have been completely reversed from that of the 50s. You know, he is June Cleaver. He stays home and does it all. The girls at work joke about it. But I've got the best husband in the world because he does the laundry, the dishes. He watches my son. He watches all the animals. And it's not as clean as I'd like it to be, because men just don't clean like women. It's that simple. But when I get home he tells me, "You've worked all day. You sit down. I'll cook." He is a super hero. – Participant 2

Finally, feelings of compassion and respect towards their partner were factors in collaboration. Participants acknowledged feeling compassion and respect for their husband's roles. These feelings created a positive bond between husband and wife and thus, fostered a partnership in division of household labor. The following quotes demonstrate the feelings of compassion and respect towards the stay-at-home father role:

Before, I was at home full-time and he worked full time. It was just kind of like a constant thing that even though I was at home all day, I couldn't get anything done. It was too much for me and I just pretty frequently would have a breakdown and just be like 'I'm so tired of just taking care of the girls all day. I can't also do laundry and dishes'. And then when I came to work full time and he decided to stay home, we kind of wanted to make the transition for him as easy as possible. I think it was, I mean, me coming to work wasn't, I don't think nearly as hard as him staying home was. I know how long his days are and I know how hard his days are." - Participant 1

We don't want it to be how in other families where the father works and the mom stays home and the father does nothing. We wanted to be more fair. It doesn't matter that just because I have a job outside the home, it doesn't mean he doesn't have a job. It's not fair that he should be working 24/7 just because he's a stay-at-home parent. I should be helping as well. Once I'm home from work, there's still work that needs to be done, and so to be fair, it shouldn't just fall on the stay-at-home parent. – Participant 8

He's been by himself most of the day with the two kids and he needs some space and some time. And so, even if I'm tired from work, I need to give him a little bit of breathing room and a little bit of space. So I think that's sort of the main factor that determines sort of how much responsibility I take in the evening, in addition to that though, I don't see the kids all day so I'm excited to see them and I want to spend time with them. Participant 20

Discussion

Division of Household Labor as a Collaborative Process

Many of the participants shared that they felt household labor continues to evolve due to the needs of their family. Some of the contributing factors were time, personal strengths and preferences, and growth of their child/ren. They shared that they felt their husbands were receptive to these needs and continued to work as a family to find a balance in the division of household labor. Many of the participants also shared that they do less household chores now that their husbands stay home than they did when they both were working. This is consistent in the findings by Barnett and Hyde (2001) who found that employed women are spending less time in child care and household tasks, whereas the men are spending more time in these areas. However, it is inconsistent with the findings by Eshleman and Bulcroft (2006), who found that women who hold nontraditional values and roles perceive the division of labor as unfair, and perceived unfairness has been related to psychological distress and marital conflict. This was inconsistent with the findings of this study in that the majority of the participants reported fairness in division of household labor and because of the fairness, they were able to spend more time with their children than doing household labor. Therefore, more participants shared positive feelings rather than distress.

Dunn, Rochlen, and O'Brien (2011) identified that the stay at home father and working mother dynamic reflected the importance of non-gender related stereotypes. They mentioned that this dynamic provided a more egalitarian lifestyle and the researchers provided a specific quote that highlighted this lifestyle as it related to household labor. It was mentioned by a participant, "My parents didn't think that a woman would ever be responsible for less than half of the housework. I'm young enough that I still enjoy proving them wrong". This is consistent in the overall finding that household labor is a collaborative process.

In regards to the subtheme of preferences and standards, Poortman and Van Der Lippe (2009) support this finding. This research explored the gendered meaning of domestic work by examining men and women's attitudes towards household labor and found that "women had more favorable attitudes towards cleaning, cooking, and child care" (2009, p 526.) This study went on to describe that the more favorable the person was towards the labor, the more they enjoyed it and felt responsible for that task. This is consistent with the current finding that the working mothers chose the responsibility of various household chores due to their own standards and were more likely to take on that responsibility.

In regards to the subthemes of supportive spousal support and feelings of compassion and respect, Kawamura and Brown (2010) validate these findings. The research by Kawamura and Brown explores the importance of 'mattering' in their relationships and how this affects the outlook of division of household labor. The research indicated that "the more wives believe they matter to their husbands, the more likely they are to report division of housework is fair, regardless of the share of housework the wives perform, time availability, relative resources, and gender role attitudes" (Kawamura & Brown, 2010, p. 976). This is consistent with the current finding that the working mothers who felt supported in their role as primary breadwinner were more likely to work with their partner in completing household chores. It is also consistent in the finding of the importance of feeling respected and valued in their role as the working mother.

Implications

The results of the study provide multiple implications for family dynamics, specific to nontraditional parenting roles. One implication worth noting is that some participants reported that they feel that society does not understand their choices and therefore they lack support for their family choices. Some discussed the lack of individual support for both themselves as the working mother as well as reported the lack of support their husbands have had trying to find social support. This is a consistent concern addressed by Latshaw (2011), as this study interviewed 40 stay-at-home fathers where many reported "difficulty being accepted into mother's playgroups or felt awkward asking mothers to hang out one-on-one, therefore, many reported spending long hours at home without other adult interaction" and thus contemplated returning to the workforce (p. 137) Expanding the research on stay-at-home fathers and working mothers can help educate families, friends, and society on ways to reduce tension between societal norms and personal decisions. This particular research can also provide education on the needs of those who choose nontraditional gender roles and how to provide support for a person in this role.

An additional implication is not minimizing the fatherhood role in a family dynamic. Promoting father involvement and its importance will help shed light on the positive aspects that a father can provide to his family. The study by Latshaw (2011) was interested in emerging forms of fatherhood and if the Census Bureau accurately accounts for the varying degrees of the definition of stay- at-home fatherhood. This study used a mixed methods approach to expand the definition to males who defined their fathering role as primary caretakers but fell outside the scope of stay-at-home fathers because they had applied for jobs, worked or earned money while staying home, or were home because of retirement or attending school. The study indicated that 1.4 million men identified themselves as primary caretakers but did not fit the Census Bureau's definition of stay-at-home father. Promoting education and better understanding on father- hood and their role as primary caretaker can help society shift their view on nontraditional parenting styles.

Limitations

There are several limitations to this study. One limitation is the specific requirements for participants. This study did not include fathers who contributed financially, or did not include families who had older or younger children. The study was also limited to married, heterosexual couples who were biological parents. Another limitation was that all participants were recruited through Internet blogs and sites, which limit participants that do not have access to Internet. Also, all blogs and sites that were used targeted a specific population, which was limited. This could have been more representative of families who are receiving more social support by being a part of a blog or group that supports these roles.

An additional limitation to a phenomenological study is that the results are not generalizable. The purpose of a phenomenological study is to explore a homogenous sample to understand their perspective. However, the limitation is that the data collected from this sample can- not be assumed to be applicable to all couples who have the stay-at-home father–working mother arrangement (Rochlen et al., 2008). The final limitation was the shortcomings associated with self-report measures (Rochlen et al., 2008). Qualitative research is not based on precise measurement but reflects the person's perception. Therefore, the reliability was a potential problem as it cannot be guaranteed every observer would come to the same conclusion of self-reports (Babbie, 2004).

Future Directions

Qualitative research regarding the stay-at-home father and working mother relationship is limited. There is a specific need to further research regarding family choices in parenting, especially nontraditional gender roles. For example, it would be beneficial to know the father's perspective regarding the family dynamics of this arrangement. This study focused solely on the mother's subjective experience. The knowledge of the father's perspective could contribute to not only awareness but also identifying the support that the fathers need.

Expanding the study to include various family dynamics is needed. Same-sex parents and blending families would be beneficial in bringing awareness to various family dynamics and its impact within the family. Studies could also be expanded to include a look into the support system within the family, such as grandparents, extended family and close friends, and the working parent's colleagues. Gaining awareness of the support, or lack thereof, would be important in helping understand how this may contribute to the well-being and satisfaction of the parents.

References

Babbie, E. (2004). The practice of social research (10th ed). Belmont, CA: Wadsworth Publishing.

Barnett, R., & Hyde, J. (2001). Women, men, work, and family: An expansionist theory. *American Psychologist*, 56(10), 781-796.

Baxter, P., & Jack, S. (2008). Qualitative case study methodology: Study design and implementation for novice researchers. *The Qualitative Report,* 13(4), 544-559.

Claffey, S. T., & Mickelson, K. D. (2009). Division of household labor and distress: The role of perceived fairness for employed mothers. *Sex Roles, 60, 819-831.*

Coltrane, S. (2010). Gender theory and household labor. *Sex Roles, 63,* 791-800.

Creswell, J. (2007). Qualitative inquiry and research design: Choosing among five approaches (2nd ed.). Thousand Oaks, CA: Sage.

Creswell, J. W. (2009). Research design: qualitative, quantitative, and mixed methods approaches (3rd ed.). Thousand Oaks, CA: Sage.

Denzin, N., & Lincoln, Y. (2003). The landscape of qualitative research (2nd ed.). Thousand Oaks, CA: Sage.

Denzin, N., & Lincoln, Y. (2013). The landscape of qualitative research (4th ed.). Thousand Oaks, CA: Sage

Dunn, M. G., Rochlen, A. B., & O'Brien, K. M. (2011). Employee, mother, and partner: An exploratory investigation of working women with stay-at-home father. *Journal of Career Development, 40*(1), 3-22.

Eshleman, J., & Bulcroft, R. (2006). The family (11th ed.). Boston, MA: Pearson.

Fischer, J., & Anderson, V. (2012). Gender role attitudes and characteristics of stay-at-home and employed fathers. *Psychology of Men & Masculinity,* 13(1), 16-31.

Glasser, W. (1998). Choice theory: A New psychology of personal freedom. New York, NY: HarperCollins.

Golafshani, N. (2003). Understanding reliability and credibility in qualitative research. *Qualitative Report,* 8, 597-607.

Latshaw, B. (2011). Is fatherhood a full time job? Mixed methods insight into measuring stay at home fatherhood. *Fathering*, 9, 125-149.

Leedy, P., & Ormrod, J. (2005). Practical research: planning and design (8th ed.). Upper Saddle River, NJ: Pearson.

Lothallar, H., Mikula, G., & Schoebi, D. (2009). What contributes to the (im)balance division of family work between the sexes? *Swiss Journal of Psychology, 68*(3), 143-152.

Kalmijn, M., & Monden, C. (2011). *Journal of Social and Personal Relationships, 29,* 358-374.

Kawamura, S., & Brown. S. L. (2010). Mattering and wives' perceived fairness of the division of household labor. *Social Science Research, 39,* 976-986.

Lively, K. J., Steelman, L. C., & Powell, B. (2010). Equity, emotion, and household division of labor response. Social Psychology Quarterly, 4, 358-379.

Meisenbach, R. (2010). The female breadwinner: Phenomenological experience and gendered identity in work/family spaces. *Sex Roles, 62,* 2-19.

Mertens, D. (2005). Research and evaluation in education and psychology: Integrating diversity with quantitative, qualitative, and mixed methods (2nd ed.). Thousand Oaks, CA: Sage.

Poortman, A., & Van Der Lippe, T. (2009). Attitudes toward housework and child care and the gendered division of labor. *Journal of Marriage and Family, 71,* 526-541.

Rehel, E. M. (2014). When dad stays home too: Paternity leave, gender, and parenting. *Gender & Society, 28*(1), 110-132.

Rochlen, A., Suizzo, M., McKelley, R., & Scaringi, V. (2008). Predictors of relationship satisfaction, psychological well-being, and life satisfaction among stay-at-home fathers. *Psychology of Men & Masculinity, 9*(1), 17-28.

Tao, W., Janzen, B., & Abonyi, S. (2010). Gender, division of unpaid family work and psychological distress in dual-earner families. *Clinical Practices & Epidemiology in Mental Health*, 6, 36-46.

U.S. Census Bureau. (2012a). Current population survey: Annual social and economic supplement. Retrieved from https://www.census.gov/hhes/www/poverty/publications/ pubs-cps.html

U.S. Census Bureau. (2012b). Profile America facts for fea- tures. Retrieved from https://www.census.gov/newsroom/releases/archives/facts_for_features_special_editions/

Wood, J., & Repetti, R. (2004). What gets dad involved? A longitudinal study of change in parental child caregiving involvement. *Journal of Family Psychology*, 18(1), 237-249.

About the Authors

Cassie Rushing, PhD, LPC-S, is an Associate Professor at Amberton University for the Professional Counseling Program. She earned her Doctorate in Counseling Studies from Capella University and her Master's degree in Forensic Psychology from the University of North Dakota. Additionally, she practices as a Licensed Professional Counselor Supervisor in the state of Texas. In her private practice, she specializes in working with children, teens, couples, and family dynamics. Her current research interests involve family dynamics and non-traditional family roles. Dr. Rushing has presented at state and international conferences on topics related to nontraditional family roles and family dynamics.

Misti Sparks, PhD, LMFT-S, is an Associate Professor of Graduate Counseling at Texas Wesleyan University. She earned her PhD and MS in Marriage and Family Therapy from Texas Woman's University. In addition, she's currently practicing as a Marriage and Family Therapist and Supervisor in the state of Texas. Her current research interests include quality of life of older adults and non-traditional family roles. Dr. Sparks has presented at state and international conferences on topics related to nontraditional family roles and quality of life of older adults.

Lisa Powell, PhD, LPC, LMFT-S, is an Adjunct Professor at NorthCentral University in the school of Marriage and Family Sciences. She earned her PhD from Amridge University in Montgomery, Alabama in Marriage and Family Therapy. Lisa has a private practice in Plano, TX, where she treats families and couples with her therapy dog, Luke. Her areas of research interests include pet therapy and therapy with non-traditional couples and families. Lisa has presented at regional and national conferences on non-traditional family counseling topics.

Clinical Metaphysical Psychology: An Approach to Reunifying Metaphysics and Psychology into a New Clinical Discipline

Blaine T. Garfolo
Northwestern Polytechnic University

ABSTRACT

Metaphysics is often viewed as the branch of philosophy concerned with the ultimate nature of reality, the universe, being and existence as a whole. In studying the etymology of the word 'psychology', one discovers it translates as "Study of the soul". Arguably, as the name Psychology implies, it was to empower a science that had, as its stated purpose, the study of the soul.

Psychologists need a frame of reference consistent with an underlying metaphysical view of human existence in order to determine the proper modality for therapeutic intervention. There are many choices that confront the psychotherapeutic practitioner ranging from Western conventional psychopharmacology and psychotherapy, to holistic and alternative modalities. Today's psychology practice, which is based on the Biomedical Model, cannot, by itself, replace the disciplines of metaphysics, ethics, philosophy, or religion (spirituality) as an effective, integrated course of treatment.

The flaw then in the modality of treatment for psychological disorders is the Biomedical Model itself and reunification of Metaphysics and Psychology (Aristotle's original concept) into the science of Metaphysical Psychology is desperately needed in order to holistically treat the 'individual'. However, how can the clinician perform this new integrative role of care provider without being provided with an integrated systems-based education? This new clinician must be knowledgeable in the dynamics of both Metaphysics and Psychology and will constitute a new Clinical Metaphysical Psychology framework. This clinician will require an understanding of the principles, concepts, and structural issues that will form the foundation of a comprehensive approach to healing, a perspective largely absent from current educational programs.

Keywords: Psychology, Metaphysics, Clinical Metaphysical Psychology, Biomedical Model, Reunification, Education, Healing, Spirituality

Introduction

The study of psychology has always been important but never more so in today's world where we are experiencing such rapid change in terms of technology and our ordinary day-to-day living. With advances in our understanding of how the conscious mind and the brain interact we have come to realize that much of our previous beliefs about how and what we think about are incorrect. Given this new understanding, the study and application of psychology is a useful tool with which to correct some of these previously held beliefs.

For Aristotle, psychology was the culmination of something he termed metaphysics and natural science and served as a foundation for his philosophy by providing a framework for understanding speech, thought and action. Aristotle's metaphysics was composed of three main branches: *Ontology* (the study of being and existence), *Universal Science* (which focused on first principles of reasoning and logic), and *Natural Theology* (concerned with the study of God, spiritual issues and the existence of the divine). If we look at the etymology of the word 'Meta' - and 'Physics', the word metaphysics is derived from the Greek words μετά (metá) (meaning "beyond" or "after") and φυσικά (physiká) (meaning "physical"), "physical". To varying degrees Aristotle's logic, rhetoric, politics and ethics all draw on these views. Metaphysics is often viewed as the branch of philosophy concerned with the ultimate nature of reality, the universe, being and existence as a whole. As such, included in the field of Metaphysics is the study of cosmology, ontology and philosophical theology.

It was Goclenius in 1590 that is credited with the invention of the term 'psychology' evolved from Aristotle's definition into an 'academic psychology' and viewed as a progression of a basic set of dominant or highly influential systems. According to May (1958), psychology "won its freedom from metaphysics" toward the latter half the nineteenth century (p. 8). That is, psychology is now a single focus, systematic study of the many ways that human beings are factually involved with each other.

If we study the etymology of the word 'psychology', one would discover that the root word of Psychology is *psyche* which, in its original Greek translation, meant 'soul'. Additionally, as the Greek translation of *'ology'* signifies *'the study of'*, it can be argued that it was Goclenius' intention (as evidenced by his word Psychology) to empower a science that had, as its stated purpose, the study of the soul.

As a metaphysician is interested in everything that is or can be; the metaphysician studies *all* reality. This means that many of the problems sometimes included in general metaphysics may conveniently be treated in the specialty parts of today's disciplines such as cosmology and psychology. But treating a problem in a sub specialization does not necessarily call into the practice knowledge of the specialty.

Metaphysics is a science and a branch of philosophy that searches for the 'science of wisdom'. Conversely, Psychology is known as the *science of the mind* and studies the interactions between thinking and behavior. Metaphysics therefore, captures the holistic and thoroughly personal nature of human existence without succumbing to the radical mind/body split that the current trend in psychology promotes.

Psychologists need a frame of reference consistent with an underlying metaphysical view of human existence. However, in order to determine the proper modality for therapeutic intervention, psychotherapists must design approaches that not only include the more 'clinical' aspects of treatment, but also ones that acknowledge the location of the client in that client's own search for meaning. There are many choices that confront the psychotherapeutic practitioner ranging from Western conventional psychopharmacology and psychotherapy, to holistic and alternative modalities, to complementary adjuncts that may be combined with conventional methods. These approaches to the achievement of mental health are parallel in their acknowledgement that mental health achieves more than the absence of mental illness. Additionally, a sound and comprehensive course of psychotherapy includes the integration and merging of the client's individual search for meaning and, if applicable, spiritual journey with sound clinical practice. It is our contention that this approach to the client and practitioner's joint search for the roots of relevant psychological and bodily suffering will increase the likelihood of discovery, resolution, and provide healing that is unique to each client. Today's psychology practice, which is based on the Biomedical Model, cannot by itself replace the disciplines of metaphysics, ethics, philosophy, or religion (spirituality) as an effective course of treatment.

It is our contention that the flaw in the mode of treatment for individuals with psychological disorders is the Biomedical Model itself. It is our belief that a reunification of Metaphysics and Psychology into the science of Metaphysical Psychology, in both theory and in practice, is desperately needed in order to holistically treat the 'individual'. Unlike the hierarchical model that characterizes the clinician/client relationship of the Biomedical Model, the relationship between clinician and patient in the Metaphysical Psychology framework would be more of a partnership relationship. However, how can the clinician perform this new integrative role of care provider without being provided with an integrated systems-based education? This new clinician must be knowledgeable in the dynamics of each of the component parts of Metaphysics and Psychology that will constitute the new Clinical Metaphysical Psychology framework. This will require an understanding of the principles, concepts, and structural issues that will form the foundation of a comprehensive approach to healing. This perspective is largely absent from current educational programs.

Background

During the 1970s medics started questioning the validity of the biomedical model. Ludwig (1975) described psychiatry as a "hodgepodge of unscientific opinions, assorted philosophies, schools of thought, mixed metaphors, propaganda, politicking for mental health and other esoteric goals" (Engel, 1977; Lanigan, 2010). However, Engle (1977), a psychiatrist, stated that he did not accept such a premise and contended that "all medicine is in crisis and that it derives from an adherence to a model of disease no longer adequate for the scientific tasks and social responsibilities of either medicine or psychiatry" (Carson, Ringbauer, & Stone, 2000; Lanigan, 2010). "Biomedicine assumes disease to be fully accounted for by deviations from the norm of measurable biological (somatic) variables and it leaves no room within its framework for psychological and social dimensions of illnesses" (Engle 1977)

By using the Biomedical model in psychiatry, the basic assumption is that psychological disorders are diseases. The nature of onset, distribution of cases, development and course, treatment response, and associated features seen in psychological disorders are seen to be parallel to what occurs in physical diseases. This model assumes diseases of any sort can be fully understood in terms of abnormal biological variables. Therefore, a 'psychological' disorder can be explained in terms of a disorder of underlying physical mechanisms (biochemical, physiological, etc.) where the biological realm is the primary source of the problem.

The Biomedical model simply cannot account for psychological disorders. The Biological model can provide an explanation that answers 'how' questions such as how a particular disease process occurred. However, the Biological model cannot provide an explanation of the 'why' questions such as why this disorder occurred. The Biological model is ***Form over Function***. For the understanding of psychopathology then, we need not look beyond the biological level. This approach embraces reductionism, a philosophical view that complex phenomena (such as thoughts, behaviors, emotions) can be completely understood and explained in terms of a more basic level. That is, in psychology, thoughts, behaviors and emotions can be 'reduced' to the more basic level of biological processes. A thought is a neurological event in the brain. Psychopathology then is a biological phenomenon. As a result, the limitations of a medical model that cannot effectively incorporate psychological, psychosocial, or spiritual factors-factors that are at the source of a number of these ailments has become increasingly evident.

Engle (1978) disputed this line of reasoning and suggested a new model - the "BioPsychoSocial" model. He proposed the need for a fundamental reorientation in scientific perspectives in order to open a way to more holistic approaches (Carson et al., 2000; Lanigan, 2010). The BioPsychoSocial model is an interdisciplinary model that assumes that health and wellness are caused by a complex interaction of biological, psychological, and sociocultural factors. The BioPsychoSocial model challenged the Biomedical model in that the underlying assumption of the Biomedical model is invalid as it is not successful at explaining some illnesses, especially the group of 'functional illnesses' that are diagnosed daily.

The Biomedical model suffers from three distinct flaws:

1. *Objectivism:* all relevant knowledge about a patient can be exclusively achieved through an impersonal assessment of sensory-based information;
2. *Determinism:* causation is exclusively characterized by an upward and linear mechanistic linkage; and
3. *Positivism:* knowledge exclusively accumulates through the growth of data from the positive results of sensory-based experimentation.

The BioPsychoSocial model, presented as a conceptual framework or theory of illness is an alternative model that acknowledges the importance of factors other than disease and suggests a systems approach to illness. The BioPsychoSocial model states that mind, body, and environment interact in causing disease. Features are interdependent and, theoretically, none has functional priority over the others. Therefore, no single illness, patient or condition can be reduced to any one aspect. They are all, more or less equally, relevant in all cases at all times otherwise there is the danger that the choice of emphasizing one aspect rather than another lies with the practitioner's subjective conviction (Ghaemi, 2008, 2010; Golden, 2004; Jaspers, 1997). The BioPsychoSocial model offers practical and professional advantages for clinical psychiatry and humanistic advantages to mental health service users.

The majority of criticisms of the BioPsychoSocial model can be summarized as:

1. How is one aspect prioritized over another?

2. There seems to be no overall theory by which to reconcile the differing approaches to the BioPsychoSocial model.
3. It is viewed as a 'general free-for-all' in patient treatment.

With respect to the BioPsychoSocial model if the clinician is to perform their new integrative role of care provider, they must be provided with an integrated systems based education. Such a clinician must be knowledgeable in the dynamics of the principles, concepts, and structural issues that underlie a comprehensive approach to healing - a perspective that is largely absent from current educational programs.

Reintegration of Ontology, Natural Theology and Universal Science Into Metaphysical Psychotherapy

The terms spirituality and religion are often used interchangeably. However, agreement on the exact definition of the terms does not exist in the literature. Spirituality is individual and self-determined, while religion involves community connections, shared beliefs and rituals. Therefore, spirituality may or may not include religion; it may find expression in a religious context or remain outside it. Spirituality is often described as the broader of the two terms and has come to refer to meaning and purpose in one's life, a search for wholeness, and a relationship with a transcendent being. For the purposes of this paper, we define spirituality within psychotherapy as "being concerned with an individual's search for meaning and purpose in their lives, as well as their development of a larger sense of belonging and community."

Because spirituality comes into focus in times of stress, suffering, physical and mental illness, loss, dying and bereavement, it is important aspect of the human condition not only in psychiatry but also throughout all of medicine. Contemporary psychotherapy has lost sight of important aspects of the human experience as well as of ways of helping people encumbered by life's difficulties. This is not surprising as psychology has had a long history of being neglectful, if not outright antagonistic, to issues related to spirituality and religion, often determining those who are spiritual or religious as being deluded or at least not as psychologically healthy and advanced as they could be. Freud (1927) called religious interests "illusions, fulfillments of the oldest, strongest and most urgent wishes of mankind". It is, therefore, understandable that clinical psychology has de-spiritualized the psychotherapeutic endeavor and has overlooked the spiritual dimensions of life and of experience.

Justification For Inclusion

The incorporation of religion and spirituality into psychological care is consistent with Aristotle's Metaphysics as his definition included matters of spirit, energy (or soul), as well as science of the mind and spirit. This reintegration does not take a dualistic approach to mind and body, but instead views this reintegration **as a multiple treatment modality; the application of several different therapeutic approaches** that the biological, the psychological, the social and the spiritual and cannot be disaggregated from the whole. To get well, we have to heal ourselves on all four levels as depicted in Figure 1.

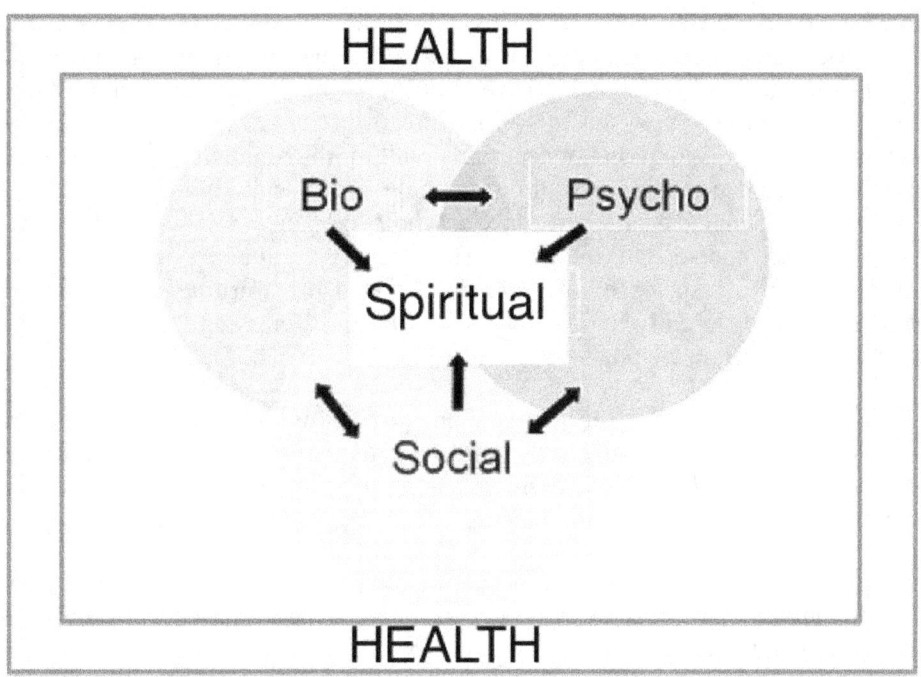

Figure 1 – The Metaphysical Aspects of Humanity

The Component Parts of the Metaphysical Aspects of Humanity are:

- The **Biological** component refers to the fact that pathogens like germs and toxins precipitate illness.
- The **Psychological**/behavioral component looks for potential psychological causes for a health problem such lack of self-control, emotional turmoil, and negative thinking.
- The **Social** component explains how different social factors such as socioeconomic status, culture, poverty, and technology can influence health.
- The **Spiritual** component looks to make sense of what is happening.

No single illness, patient or condition can be reduced to any one aspect. They are all, more or less equally, relevant, in all cases, at all times. (Ghaemi, 2008, 2009; Golden, 2004; Jaspers, 1997)

Our Human Makeup

There are four parts to our human being: emotional, mental, physical and spiritual. The emotional part is our heart (our feelings); the mental part is our mind or brain (our thoughts); the physical part is our body - what we can see and touch; and the spiritual part is our whole being, our whole self (or what we can sense). If we are to get well, we must get well on all four levels.

When one of the four parts of our being is out of balance, the rest is out of balance as well. Disease can be understood as a disturbance in the balance of the relationship between the biological, psychological, social and spiritual dimensions of our makeup. Humans are intrinsically spiritual since all persons are in relationship with themselves, others, nature, and the significant or sacred and everyone has a spiritual history (Carson et al., 2000; Lanigan, 2010). For many people, this spiritual history unfolds within the context of an explicit religious tradition; for others it unfolds as a set of philosophical principles or significant experiences. This spiritual history helps shape each patient as a whole person. When life-threatening illness strikes, it strikes each person in totality. This totality includes not simply the biologic, psychological, and social aspects of the person, but also the spiritual aspects as well. Each aspect can be affected differently by a person's history and illness and each aspect can interact and affect other aspects of the person.

For example, if you break your leg in an accident, **physically** you are hurt. **Emotionally**, you might be shocked or upset. **Mentally** you might find it frustrating because you cannot do what you would normally do. **Spiritually**, you might ask yourself why it happened - we often look for answers or reasons as to why something happens.

It often happens that people entering into psychotherapy truly want to engage in the process of self-exploration, but they also attempt to avoid certain embarrassing aspects of their private lives. They want the psychotherapist to like them, not be disgusted by the ugliness lurking in the shadows of their personalities. Often they will do almost anything to hide their raw feelings of anger and betrayal resulting from past emotional wounds. The psychotherapist has to determine a course of 'healing' to bring about the complete recovery of the client.

Healing is generally referred to as regaining physical health, and there are many ways to go about it, ranging from traditional Western scientific medicine to alternative herbal and holistic methods. But being physically healthy is only one facet of your being; having peace of mind (mental healing or mental health) is another thing entirely. Mental health is much more than the absence of mental illness. If psychotherapy is to achieve ultimate success, it must lead you into deeper level of healing, a spiritual level of psychological healing, especially after the oppressive psychological weight of a traumatic event. Spirituality is often viewed as 'the forgotten dimension' of mental health care.

A Uniform Approach

The practice of utilizing multiple treatment modalities to the same medical problem provides maximum benefit to the patient. One of the primary benefits is that all facets of the problem are addressed in a more comprehensive manner than is possible with a single treatment. Another benefit is that the patient is treated in a more holistic manner; secondary issues such as the psychological impact of illness are also treated. Treating a problem with several distinct therapeutic approaches often increases the probability of positive outcomes for the patient. Each patient is a unique individual who experiences illness differently. An additional benefit of utilizing multiple treatment modalities is the ability to customize the patient's plan of care to accommodate these variations.

The case for the Metaphysical Psychology Framework has become strengthened, in our opinion, as the combination of pharmacotherapy and standard psychotherapy appears increasingly inadequate as a solution to most patients' problems. It is becoming increasingly evident that psychiatry should offer holistic care in a primary care setting. The Metaphysical Psychology Framework is an integrative approach in which several different therapeutic techniques are used to address a patient's psychological issues. Practitioners who offer integrative therapy have a broad field of knowledge to draw upon usually requiring extensive training.

If we look at the Metaphysical Psychology Framework as an integrative therapy, the key is in the understanding that each individual person is unique and distinctive, which means that a one-size-fits all approach to therapy will not be effective. Practitioners who utilize integrative therapy can develop a program which has been designed specifically for the patient's unique needs, addressing peculiarities of the patient's personality, belief system and situation rather than providing generic treatment which may be less effective.

Properly implemented, the Metaphysical Psychology framework should:

1. Encompass all factors that relate to illness in some way.

2. Explain or predict all illnesses, especially functional illness.

3. Improve clinical management of individual patients through allowing a better analysis and understanding of the patient to include both bodily and mental domains.

Modification

Given the complexity of psychological distress, one may argue that a reasonable course of treatment involves a multi-dimensional approach. However, clinical practitioners are struggling with bringing this multidimensional perspective into their clinical assessments. To help in the assessment of complex medical problems, Huyse, et al. (1999) built on the **BioPsychoSocial framework** of Engle (1978) and developed INTERMED. INTERMED is a decision-support approach to clinical assessment that consists of a four-dimensional grid for assessment and treatment of complex psychiatric consultation cases which embodies an interdisciplinary format and allows for communication and a comprehensive understanding of the patient's condition. The strength of the psychological assessment process utilizing INTERMED stems from its comprehensive scientific methodology.

In INTERMED, the risk factors are defined within the context of a grid that includes four rows reflecting the Biological, Psychological, Social, and Health Care Systems (Davidson et al., 2004; Koenig, 2004) (refer figure 2).

Domain	History	Current state	Prognoses
Biological	Chronicity	Severity of illness	Complications and life threat
	Diagnostic complexity	Clarity of diagnostic profile	
Psychological	Restrictions in coping	Psychological adjustment to illness	Mental health threat
	Premorbid level of psychiatric dysfunction	Severity of psychiatric symptoms	
Social	Family disruption	Residential instability	Social vulnerability
	Impairment of social support	Vocational impairment	
Health Care	Intensity of prior treatment	Resistance to treatment	Care needs
	Prior treatment experience	Relation with and access to health care	

Figure 2 – INTERMED assessment grid.

One of the criticisms of the **BioPsychoSocial** model was that it did not have a clear path for implementation. INTERMED strengthened the **BioPsychoSocial** model and help satisfy this requirement as it uses a standardized assessment, adds structure, targets a clear outcome and enhances the effectiveness of the patient-doctor relationship. INTERMED addresses the importance of comprehensive assessment and draws attention to complex factors influencing outcomes of biomedical treatments in medical patients. However, although the INTERMED strengthened **BioPsychoSocial** model has shown promise the magnitude of successful patient outcomes was often limited, and remission rarely achieved.

Modification of the Intermed Grid

Adding a spiritual approach as a fifth domain to the INTERMED grid could address the limitations of the **BioPsychoSocial** model by:

1. Providing a sense of safety in processing thoughts and feelings;
2. Resolving the troubling aspects of the memories of the traumatic experience;
3. Integrating positive growth into the patient's lifestyle and
4. Including a program of spirituality and meditation that heals the root of suffering in its origin by working through bodily and psychological suffering in a spiritually grounded way (Chambless & Ollendick, 2001; Huyse et al., 1999; Koenig, 2004; Mills, 2002; Sloan, Bagiella, & Powell, 1999; Williams, Holmbeck, & Greenly, 2002).

By promoting the integration of Spirituality into the BioPsychoSocial model, the modified model will allow the clinician to provide medical care that will:

1. Look at the factors that are of importance in determining whether a person is ill or not.
2. Specify the nature of the inter-relationships between these factors and being ill.

3. Identify the major factors relevant to the causation and understanding of illness.
4. Predict or explain observed inter-relationships and other phenomena concerning illness.
5. Acknowledge explicitly the perceptions and experiences of the ill person (i.e. be person-centered).
6. Acknowledge choice or free will in the understanding of the illness.
7. Recognize that well-being or quality of life influences recovery.
8. Will correlate the patient's religious beliefs with health beliefs and address their individual spiritual needs and provide a course of treatment that is in agreement with their belief system.
9. Consist of the integration of spiritual wisdom combined with sound clinical practice to help us heal ourselves and others from the roots of psychological and bodily suffering (Ganje-Fling & McCathy, 1991; Hill & Pargament, 2003; Huyse et al., 1999; Koenig, 2004; Mills, 2002; Plante & Sherman, 2001; Sloan et al., 1999; Wade, 2009).

If medical professionals take the position that spirituality preserves identity and sense of self, then professional practice assessments will be made within a framework that matters to the patient. This means identifying spiritual needs and resources in ways that:

1. Respect a patient's belief system without infringing or 'converting' them;
2. Involve all members of the care giving team to utilize their unique contributions to the patient's care including a spiritual perspective;
3. Integrate a comprehensive treatment strategy that is understood by all members of the care giving team;
4. Provide the ability for religious care outside of spiritual care. While spiritual care in general may be provided by the care giving team, specific religious care is best provided by a person from the same faith community, preferably one willing to participate in the care giving team.

We propose that the INTERMED grid be modified (refer figure 3) to include a spiritual component that would strengthen not only INTERMED but would provide the necessary assessment structure to complete a Metaphysical Psychology framework of patient care. The new INTERMED domain would be Spirituality and the added areas of Spiritual/Religious assessment would allow for the examination of:

1. Religiosity
2. Spiritual Identity
3. Spiritual Needs
4. Spiritual Well-Being
5. Spiritual/Religious Coping and Support

Domain	History	Current State	Prognoses
Biological	Chronicity Diagnostic Complexity	Severity of Illness Clarity of diagnostic profile	Complications and life threat
Psychological	Restrictions In Coping Premorbid Level of psychiatric dysfunction	Psychological adjustment to illness Severity of psychiatric symptoms	Mental health threat
Social	Family disruption Impairment of Social Support	Residential instability Vocational Impairment	Social Vulnerability
Health Care	Intensity of prior treatment Prior treatment experience	Resistance to treatment Relation with and access to health care	Care needs
Spiritualism	Religiosity Spiritual Identity	Spiritual need Spiritual Well Being	Spiritual/Religious Coping and Support

Figure 3 – Metaphysical Psychology INTERMED assessment grid.

This addition would allow the clinician, in a Spiritual problem-solving style, the ability to perform a Spiritual History (a Spiritual Appraisal) as part of the patient record of treatment. The Spiritual History should be communicated and documented in patient records. The goals of the Spiritual History would be to:

1. Invite the patient to share spiritual and religious beliefs, and to define what spirituality is for them and their spiritual goals.
2. Learn about the patient's beliefs and values.
3. Assess their level of spiritual distress as well as to determine sources of spiritual strength.
4. Empower the patient to find inner resources of healing and acceptance.
5. Identify spiritual and religious beliefs that might affect the patient's health care decision-making.
6. Identify spiritual practices that might be helpful in the treatment or care plan.
7. Identify patients who need referral to a board-certified chaplain or other spiritual care provider (Huyse et al., 1999; Koenig, 2004; Mills, 2002; Sloan et al., 1999).

Follow-up spiritual histories or assessments should be conducted for all patients whose medical, psychosocial, or spiritual condition changes and as part of routine follow-up in a medical history.

The typical patient treatment plan would consist of the following four component parts:

1. Physical assessment
2. Psychological assessment
3. Social: family support assessment
4. Spiritual: Faith assessment

The **Metaphysical Psychology** framework emphasizes the need to view patients not simply as biological creatures, but as physical, psychological, social, and spiritual beings so that they may be effectively treated and healed as whole persons.

Steps to Implementation

By integrating the Spiritual component into the **Metaphysical Psychology** framework we are able to:

1. Develop a therapeutic alliance that is sensitive to the spiritual dimension.
2. Maintain the therapeutic alliance and deal with spiritual transference, countertransference, alliance ruptures, ambivalence and resistance.
3. Perform assessment and diagnostics include the spiritual dimension.
4. Incorporate spiritual and psychological interventions.
5. Undertake training with religious/spiritual resources if needed.
6. Monitor and evaluate overall treatment progress and outcomes on all dimensions including spiritual.
7. Incorporate the spiritual dimension in the termination process.

To properly integrate the **Metaphysical Psychology** framework into a cohesive treatment modality that properly emphasizes biological, psychological, social, and spiritual aspects of our being, our implementation should be approached in phases.

Phase 1:

1. Engagement: forming a trusting relationship with a therapist
2. Stabilization: reducing dangerous behaviors
3. Psycho-education: educating the patient about the causes and symptoms of their diagnosis.
4. Determining the social/family support mechanism in place (if any) to aid in recovery.

Phase 2:

Work with a variety of professional practitioners that can contribute to the therapy by way of:

1. Body-oriented psychotherapies
2. Existential psychotherapies
3. Phenomenological psychotherapies
4. Transpersonal psychotherapies
5. Integrative psychotherapies
6. Expressive art psychotherapies
7. Multi-modal psychotherapies.

Phase 3:

The final phase focuses on improving the person's quality of life, by increasing engagement in spirituality or other sources of meaning and fulfillment.

1. Inquiring if they "consider themself spiritual or religious and if they have spiritual beliefs that help cope with stress?"
2. Determining what importance faith or beliefs have in their life and have their beliefs influenced how they have cared for themselves during this illness? Additionally, what role do their beliefs play in regaining their health?
3. Determining how they would like the healthcare provider to address these issues in their healthcare. That is, should the health care provider consider spiritual needs to be addressed in their course of treatment?

Final Thoughts

Metaphysics and its interface with medicine have been extensively discussed in this paper and should be considered by all health professionals. Patient care, previously limited only to the biology dimension, should now formally expanded to other dimensions with a more integrative and complex approach including an awareness of spiritual beliefs/needs of their patients. It is hoped that the approach to the reunification of Metaphysics and Psychology, as discussed in this paper, will be increasingly incorporated into psychotherapeutic practice in the near future.

For a proper integration, formal training and practical experience will be necessary as it is not possible for therapists to learn such techniques through course work alone. Perhaps through extensive workshops and retreats where therapists participate in spiritual disciplines that involve extensive commitment to learning about such skills and approaches will provide the framework for proper integration.

By utilizing the approach outlined in this paper, clinical practices can integrate all the dimensions necessary for a **Clinical Metaphysical Psychology** practice. Developing inter-professional training programs, engaging community clergy and spiritual leaders in the care of patients and families, promoting professional development that incorporates a Metaphysical Psychology framework and developing accountability measures will ensure that the holistic care of a patient is fully integrated into a patient's care plan. Depending on how these and related concerns are resolved, it is possible that empirically validated, Metaphysical-oriented integrative psychotherapeutic forms will emerge within the contemporary western framework of patient care.

It is hoped that as a result of our framework, it will be possible for health professionals, including those responsible for primary care whose training and experience were previously limited only to the biology dimension, can now accept a psychotherapeutic modality as one being expanded to other dimensions in a more integrative and rational way. If psychology is to progress and grow as a discipline, the incorporation of the biological, social, psychological, and spiritual dimensions of the human existence into an integrated discipline *'Clinical Metaphysical Psychology'* is essential in the treatment of patients from a multicultural and diverse society.

References

A., Yeheskel, A., & Herman, J. (2005). The BioPsychoSocial model: Have we made any progress since 1977? Families, Systems, & Health, 23(4), 379-386.

Ader, R. & Brown, T. (2004). The BioPsychoSocial model: Interdisciplinarity inscience and medicine. Jur Rochester, 3(1), 1-9.

Ahn Y. J., McInnes Miller M., Can MFTs Address Spirituality with Clients in Publically Funded Agencies?, *Contemporary Family Therapy*, 32, 102-116, 2010

Avery, A., King, S., Bretherton, R., & Ørner, R. (1999). Deconstructing psychological debriefing and the emergence of calls for evidence-based practice. Traumatic Stress Points, 13, 2.

Barsky AJ, Borus JF Functional Somatic Syndromes. Annals of Internal Medicine 1999;130:910-921

Baum, A. & Posluszny, D. M. (1999). Health psychology: Mapping biobehavioral contributions to health and illness. Annual Review of Psychology, 1999.

Bennett MR, Hacker PMS Philosophical foundations of neuroscience. Blackwell publishing, Oxford 2003

Borrell-Carrió F, Suchman AL, Epstein RM: The BioPsychoSocial model 25 years later: principles, practice, and scientific inquiry. Ann Fam Med 2004;2:576-582.

Borrell-Carrio, F., Suchman, A. L., & Epstein. R. M. (2004). The BioPsychoSocial model 25 years later: Principles, practice, and scientific inquiry. Annals of Family Medicine, 2(6), 576-582.

Buchbinder R, Jolley D, Wyatt M. Population based intervention to change back pain beliefs and disability: three part evaluation. British Medical Journal 2001; 322:1516–20

Campbell W, Rohrbaugh R. The BioPsychoSocial Formulation Manual. Routledge, 2006.

Carson AJ, Ringbauer B, Stone J, et al. Do medically unexplained symptoms matter? A prospective cohort of 300 new referrals to neurology outpatient clinics. J Neurol Neurosurg Psychiatry 2000;68:207–10

Chambless, D. L., & Ollendick, T. H. (2001). Empirically supported psychological interventions: Controversies and evidence. *Annual Review of Psychology, 52,* 685–716.

Cohen J, Brown Clark S: John Romano and George Engel: Their Lives and Work.University of Rochester Press, Rochester, NY, and Boydell and Brewer Limited, Suffolk UK, 2010.

Craddock N, Antebi D, Attenburrow MJ, Bailey A, Carson A, Cowen P, et al. Wake-up call for British psychiatry. Br J Psychiatry 2008; 193: 6– 9.

Craig P, Dieppe P, Macintyre S, Michie S, Nazareth I, Petticrew M Developing and evaluating complex interventions: the new Medical Research Council guidance BMJ 2008;337:a1655,   doi: 10.1136/bmj.a1655 de Jonge P , Stiefel F Internal consistency of the INTERMED in patients with somatic diseases. Journal of Psychosomatic Research 2003;54:497-499

de Jonge P, Huyse FJ, Slaets JP, Söllner W, Stiefel FC Operationalization of BioPsychoSocial case complexity in general health care: the INTER- MED project. Aust N Z J Psychiatry. 2005;39:795-9

de Jonge P, Maarten-Friso Ruinemans G, Huyse FJ, ter Wee PM A simple risk score predicts poor quality of life and non-survival at 1 year follow-up in di- alysis patients Nephrology Dialysis Transplantation 2003;18:2622-2628

Demertzi A, Liew C, Ledoux D, Bruno MA, Sharpe M, Laureys S, Zeman A Dualism persists in the science of mind. Annals of New York Academy of Science 2009;1157:1-9

Disler PB, Wade DT Should all stroke rehabilitation be home based? Am J Phys Med Rehabil 2003;82:733–735.

Eck, B. E. (2002). An exploration of the therapeutic use of spiritual disciplines in clinical practice. *Journal of Psychology and Christianity, 21,* 266–280.

Engel GL The Need for a New Medical Model: A Challenge for Biomedicine Science 1977;196:129-136

Engel GL. The BioPsychoSocial model and the education of health professionals. Ann N Y Acad Sci 1978; 310: 169– 87.

Engel GL. The need for a new medical model: a challenge for biomedicine. Science 1977; 196: 129– 36.

Engel, G. (1968). A life setting conducive to illness: The giving-up—given-up complex. Annals of Internal Medicine, 69(2).

Engel, G. (1972). Must we precipitate a crisis in medical education to solve the crisis in health care? Annals of Internal Medicine, 76, 487-490.

Engel, G. (1973). Enduring attributes of medicine relevant for the education of the physician. Annals of Internal Medicine, 78, 587-593.

Engel, G. (1976). The predictive value of psychological variables for disease and death. Annals of Internal Medicine, 85,(5).

Engel, G. (1989). A response from george engel to joseph herman. Families, Systems, & Health, 23(4), 377-378

Engel, P. A. (2001) George l. engel: Remembering his life and work; rediscovering his soul. Psychosomatics, 42, 94-99.

Ferguson E, Cassaday HJ, Erskind J, Delahaye G Individual differences in the temporal variability of medically unexplained symptoms reporting. British Journal of Health Psychology   2004;9:219 – 240

Fink, P. J. (2004). The BioPsychoSocial approach: A review. The Permanente Journal, 8(3).

Fiscella, K. (2005). George engel storytelling. Families, Systems, & Health, 23(4), 410-412.

Foa, E. B., Keane, T. M., & Friedman, M. J. (Eds.). (2000). Effective Treatments for PTSD: Practice Guidelines from the International Society for Traumatic Stress Studies. New York: Guilford Publications.

Frankel RM, Quill TE, McDaniel SH (Eds.): The BioPsychoSocial Approach: Past, Present, Future.University of Rochester Press, Rochester, NY, 2003.

Frankel, R. M., Quill, T. E., & McDaniel, S. H. (2003). The BioPsychoSocial approach: Past, present, future. University of Rochester Press.

Freud, Sigmund *The Future of an Illusion.* New York and London: W.W. Norton & Company, 1961 (1927).

Friedman, M. J. (2000). A guide to the literature on pharmacotherapy for PTSD. PTSD Research Quarterly, 11, 1.

Ganje-Fling, M. A., & McCarthy, P. R. (1991). A comparative analysis of spiritual direction and psychotherapy. *Journal of Psychology and Theology, 19,* 103–117.

Ghaemi N. The rise and fall of the BioPsychoSocial model. BrJ Psychiatry 2009; 195: 3-4

Ghaemi SN. The Concepts of Psychiatry: A Pluralistic Approach to the Mind and Mental Illness. Johns Hopkins University Press, 2007.

Ghaemi SN. Toward a Hippocratic psychopharmacology. Can J Psychiatry 2008; 53: 189– 96.

Golden R. A history of William Osler's The principles and practice of medicine. Osler Library studies in the history of medicine No. 8. Montreal, McGill University, 2004.

Grinker Sr RR. A struggle for eclecticism. Am J Psychiatry 1964; 121: 451– 7.

Hall, M. E. L., & Hall, T. W. (1997). Integration in the therapy room: An overview of the literature. *Journal of Psychology and Theology, 25,* 86–101.

Hamama-Raz, Y., Solomon, Z., Cohen, A., & Laufer, A. (2008). PTSD symptoms, forgiveness, and revenge among Israeli Palestinian and Jewish Adolescents. Journal of Traumatic Stress, 21, 521–529.

Han J, Zhu Y, Li S, Zhang J, Cheng X, Van den Berg O, Van de Woestijne KP The language of medically unexplained dyspnoea. Chest 2008;133:961-968

Haug I. E., Including a spiritual dimension in family therapy: Ethical considerations, *Contemporary Family Therapy*, 20(2), 181-194, 1998

Hepworth, J. & Cushman, R. (2005). BioPsychoSocial: Essential but not sufficient. Families, Systems, & Health, 23(4), 406-409.

Hill, P., & Pargament, K. I. (2003). Advances in the conceptualization and measurement of religion and spirituality: Implications for physical and mental health research. American Psychologist, 58, 64–

74.

Hoffman FH, Steiger WA, Magran L The Contribution of the Psychiatrist to the Comprehensive Approach in Medicine Psychosomatics 1960;1:249-253

Hoogervorst ELJ, de Jonge P, Jelles B, Huyse FJ, Heeres I, van der Ploeg HM, Uitdehaag BMJ, Polman CH The INTERMED: a screening instrument to identify multiple sclerosis patients in need of multidisciplinary treatment. Journal Neurology Neurosurgery and Psychiatry 2003;74:20-24

Huyse FJ, Lyons JS, Stiefel FC, Slaets JPJ. De Jonge P, Fink P, Gans ROB, Guex P, Herzog T, Lobo A, Smith GC, van Schijndel RS "INTERMED": a method to assess health service need. I. Development and reliability. General Hospital Psychiatry 1999;21:39-48

Jaspers K. General Psychopathology - Volumes 1 & 2. translated by Hoenig J.and Hamilton MW. Johns Hopkins University Press, 1997

Jørgensen KJ, Gøtzsche PC Over diagnosis in publicly organized mammography screening programs: systematic review of incidence trends BMJ 2009;339:b2587, doi: 10.1136/bmj.b2587

Keefe, F. J. & Blumenthal, J. A. (2004). Health psychology: What will the future bring? Health Psychology, 23(2), 156-157.

Koenig H. G., Religion, spirituality, and medicine: research findings and implications for clinical practice, *Southern Medical Journal*, 97(12): 1194-1200, 2004

Linley, P. A., Joseph, S. (2004). Positive change following trauma and adversity: A review. Journal of Traumatic Stress, 17, 11–21.

Ludwig von Bertalanffy General System theory: Foundations, Development, Applications. New York: George Braziller, 1968 (revised edition 1976): ISBN 0-8076-0453-4

Luthy C, Cedraschi C, Rutschmann OT, Kossovsky MP, Allaz AF Managing post-acute hospital care: a case for BioPsychoSocial needs. Journal of Psychosomatic Research 2007;62:513-519

Marshall JC, Halligan PW, Fink GR, Wade DT, Frackowiak RSJ The functional anatomy of a hysterical paralysis. Cognition 1997;64:B1-B8

Matlow AG, Wright JG, Zimmerman B, Thomson K, Valente M How can the principles of complexity science be applied to improve the coordination of care for complex pediatric patients? Quality and Safety in Health Care 2006;15:85-88

Mauksch, L. (2005). But first, training in BioPsychoSocial care: A commentary on "the BioPsychoSocial model is shrink wrapped, on the shelf, ready to be used, but waiting for a new process of care". Families, Systems, & Health, 23(4), 448-449.

McMinn, M. R., & McRay, B. W. (1997). Spiritual disciplines and the practice of integration: Possibilities and challenges for Christian psychologists. *Journal of Psychology and Theology, 25,* 102–110.

McNally, R. J. (1999). Research on Eye Movement Desensitization and Reprocessing (EMDR) as a treatment for PTSD. PTSD Research Quarterly, 10, 1.

Menninger RW Psychiatry 1976: time for a holistic medicine. Annals of Internal Medicine 1976;84:603-604

Mental Health Net: Self-help Trauma, PTSD, and Stress Resources is a comprehensive listing of trauma, PTSD, and stress information and self-help resources online.

Mills, P. J. (2002). Spirituality, religiousness, and health: From research to clinical practice. *Annals of Behavioral Medicine, 24* (1), 1–2.

Moon, G. W. (1997b). Training tomorrow's integrators in today's busy intersection: Better look four ways before crossing. *Journal of Psychology and Theology, 25,* 284–293.

Nagi SZ,. An epidemiology of disability among adults in the United States. Milbank Mem Fund Q Health Soc. 1976;54:439-467

Nelson, A. A., & Wilson, W. P. (1984). The ethics of sharing religious faith in psychotherapy. *Journal of Psychology and Theology, 12,* 15–23.

Osler W. Aequanimitas (3rd edn). The Blakiston Company, 1932.

Pargament K. I., Murray-Swank N. A., Tarakeshwar N., An empirically-based rationale for a spiritually-integrated psychotherapy, *Mental Health, Religion, and Culture*, 8, 155- 165, 2005

Plante, T. G. (2007). Integrating spirituality and psychotherapy: Ethical issues and principles to consider. *Journal of Clinical Psychology, 63,* 891-902.

Plante, T. G., & Sherman, A. S. (Eds.). (2001). Faith and health: Psychological perspectives. New York: Guilford Press.

Propst L. R., Ostrom R., Watkins P., Dean T., Mashburn D., Comparative efficacy of religious and nonreligious cognitive behavioral therapy for the treatment of clinical depression in religious individuals, *Journal of Consulting and Clinical Psychology*, 60, 94-103, 1992

Richards, P. S., & Potts, W. (1995). Using spiritual interventions in psychotherapy: Practices, successes, failures, and ethical concerns of Mormon psychotherapists. *Professional Psychology: Research and Practice, 26,* 163–170.

Rose, E. M., Westefeld, J. S., & Ansley, T. N. (2001). Spiritual issues in counseling: Clients' beliefs and preferences. *Journal of Counseling Psychology, 48,* 61–71.

Russell, S. R., & Yarhouse, M. A. (2006). Religion/spirituality within APA-accredited psychology predoctoral internships. Professional Psychology: Research and Practice, 37, 430–436.

Scerri M, de Goumoëns P, Fritsch C, Van Melle G, Stiefel F, So A The INTERMED questionnaire for predicting return to work after a multidisciplinary rehabilitation program for chronic low back pain Joint Bone Spine 2006;73:736-741

Scherger, J. (2005). The BioPsychoSocial model is shrink wrapped, on the shelf, ready to be used, but waiting for a new process of care. Families, Systems, & Health, 23(4), 444-447.

Schnurr, P. P. (1999). Control groups in psychotherapy research. PTSD Research Quarterly, 10, 1.

Schultz, D. P., & Schultz, S. E. (2004). A history of modern psychology (8th ed.). Belmont, CA: Wadsworth/Thompson.

Schwabe M, Howell SJ, Reuber M Differential diagnosis of seizure disorders: A conversation analytic approach. Social Science and Medicine 2007;65:712-724

Seaburn, D. B. (2005). Is going "too far" enough? Families, Systems, & Health, 23(4), 396-399.

Shah P , Mountain D The medical model is dead - long live the medical model. British Journal of Psychiatry 2007;191:375-377

Shiell A, Hawe P , Gold L Complex interventions or complex systems? Implications for health economic evaluation BMJ 2008;336:1281-1283

Shorter E. The history of the BioPsychoSocial approach in medicine: before and after Engel. In BioPsychoSocial Medicine: An Integrated Approach to Understanding Illness (ed., P White): 1– 19. Oxford University Press, 2005

Sloan, R. P., & Bagiella, E. (2002). Claims about religious involvement and health outcomes. *Annals of Behavioral Medicine, 24* (1), 14–21.

Sloan, R. P., Bagiella, E., & Powell, T. (1999). Religion, spirituality, and medicine. The Lancet, 353, 664–667.

Smith, T. W. & Suls, J. (2004). Introduction to the special section on the future of health psychology. Health Psychology, 23(2), 115-118.

Sotile, W. M. (2005). BioPsychoSocial care of heart patients: Are we practicing what we preach? Families, Systems, & Health, 23(4), 400-403.

Spenckens AEM, Van Hemert AM, Bolk AM, Roojimans HG, Hengveld MW Unexplained physical symptoms: outcome, utilization of medical care and associated factors Psychological Medicine 1996;26:745-752

Spenkens AEM, van Hemert AM, Spinhoven P, Hawton KE, Bolk JH, Roojimans HGM Cognitive behavioural therapy for medically unexplained physical symptoms: randomised controlled trial. British Medical Journal 1995;311:1328-1332

Stark JR, Mucci L, Rothman KJ, Adami HO Prostate cancer screening: the controversy continues. BMJ 2009;339:b3601

Stein, H. F. (2005). It ain't necessarily so: The many faces of the BioPsychoSocial model. Families, Systems, & Health, 23(4), 440-443.

Stichting INTERMED Foundation

Stiefel F, Zdrojewski C, Bel Hadj F, Boffa D, Dorogi Y, So A, Ruiz J, de Jonge P Effects of a multifaceted psychiatric intervention targeted for the complex medically ill: a randomized controlled trial. Psychotherapy and Psychosomatics 2008;77:247-256

Stiefel FC, De Jonge P, Huyse FJ, Guex P, Slaets JPJ. Lyons JS, Spagnoli J, Vannotti M "INTERMED": a method to assess health service need. II. Results on its validity and clinical use. General Hospital Psychiatry 1999;21:49-56

Stier-Jarmer M, Cieza A, Borchers M, Stucki G How to apply the ICF and ICF core sets for low back pain Clinical Journal of Pain 2009;25:29-38

Stone J Functional symptoms in neurology. Practical Neurology 2009; 9:179-189. doi:10.1136/jnnp.2009.177204

Tan, S.-Y. (1994). Ethical considerations in religious psychotherapy: Potential pitfalls and unique resources. *Journal of Psychology and Theology, 22,* 389–394.

Tan, S.-Y. (1996a). Practicing the presence of God: The work of Richard J. Foster and its applications to psychotherapeutic practice. *Journal of Psychology and Christianity, 15,* 17–28.

Tedeschi, R. G., Calhoun, L. G. (1996). The Posttraumatic Growth Inventory: Measuring the positive legacy of trauma. Journal of Traumatic Stress, 9, 455–471.

The National Center for PTSD provides information about PTSD research and a PILOTS database linked to the world's largest collection of traumatic stress literature.

Trauma Information Pages provides a comprehensive listing of trauma support info, disaster info, and related mental health issues on the Internet.

Uhlig T, Moe R, Reinsberg S, Kvien TK, Cieza A, Stucki G Responsiveness of the International Classification of Functioning, Disability and Health (ICF) Core Set for rheumatoid arthritis Annals of the Rheumatic Diseases 2009;68: 879-884

Vahtera J, Kivimäki M, Forma P, Wikström J, Halmeenmäki T, Linna A, Pentti J Organizational downsizing as a predictor of disability pension: the 10-town prospective cohort study. Journal of Epidemiology and Community Health 2005;59:238-242

Van Hemert AM, Hengeveld MW, Bolk JH, Roojimans HGM, Vandenbrouke JP Psychiatric disorders in relation to medical illness among patients of a general medical clinic. Psychological Medicine 1993;23:167-173

Vermeer SE, Longstreth WT, Koudstaal PJ Silent brain infarcts: a systematic review. Lancet Neurology 2007;6:611-619

Wade DT Community rehabilitation, or rehabilitation in the community? Disability and Rehabilitation 2003;25:875-881

Wade DT Principles of Neurological Rehabilitation In: Brain's Diseases of the Nervous System. 12th Edition; (Chapter six; pp165-179) Ed: Donaghy M Oxford University Press 2009

Wade DT Selection criteria for rehabilitation services Clinical Rehabilitation 2003;17:115-118

Wade DT Social context as a focus for rehabilitation Clinical Rehabilitation 2001;15:459-461

Wade DT Why *physical* medicine, *physical* disability and *physical* rehabilitation? We should abandon Cartesian dualism. Clinical Rehabilitation 2006;20:185-190

Wade DT, Halligan PW Do biomedical models of illness make for good healthcare systems? British Medical Journal 2004;329:1398-1401

Wade DT, Halligan PW Social roles and long-term illness; is it time to rehabilitation convalescence? Clinical Rehabilitation 2007;21:291-298

Wallman KE, Morton AR, Goodman C, Grove R, Guilfoyle AM Randomized controlled trial of graded exercise in chronic fatigue syndrome Medical Journal of Australia 2004;180:444-448

Waters, D. (2005). On the "split model": So what else is new? Families, Systems, & Health, 23(4), 404-405

Waysman, M., Schwarzwald, J., & Solomon, Z. (2001). Hardiness: An examination of its relationship with positive and negative long term changes following trauma. Journal of Traumatic Stress, 14, 531–547.

Wessely S, Nimnuan C, Sharpe M Functional somatic syndromes: one or many? Lancet 1999;354:936-939

Williams, P. G., Holmbeck, G. N., & Greenly, R. N. (2002). Adolescent health psychology. Journal of Consulting and Clinical Psychology, 70(3), 828- 842. Retrieved January 12, 2007 from PsychArticles.

About the Author

Blaine Thomas Garfolo, PhD is an emeritus Associate Professor and currently serves as Chair of the DBA Advisory Committee at Northwestern Polytechnic University and is an Assessment Coordinator at the University of Phoenix in the Office of Assessment. He has taught internationally in Australia and New Zealand and was chair of Faculty Research in the COB at Prince Mohammad bin Fahd University, Saudi Arabia. He presents and publishes nationally and internationally in the fields of Assessment, Business, Psychology, Philosophy and Metaphysics.

Irreducible Social Properties: Lessons from Philosophy of Mind

Todd Jones
University of Nevada - Las Vegas

ABSTRACT

Since the beginnings of the social sciences, many social scientists have held that one of the essential *raison d'etres* for having *social* sciences is that many social activities cannot be explained in terms of the behavior of individuals. To think about how well this common anti-reductionist attitude has served the social scientists, it is very instructive to compare the anti-reductionism of the *social sciences* to anti-reductionist attitudes in the *philosophy of mind* where issues of reductionism and anti-reductionism have long been discussed at a very high level of refinement and sophistication. I argue here that the lesson we should take is that there is no clear reason to believe there the proposed irreducible properties really exist – not in the mental realm and not in the social realm.

Keywords: Irreducible, autonomous

Introduction

Since the beginnings of the social sciences, many social scientists have held that one of the essential raison d'etres for having *social* sciences is that many social activities cannot be explained in terms of the behavior of individuals. Generations of humanities-oriented social theorists (especially European ones) from Hegel (1807/1977) onward have believed that truly understanding social phenomena requires abandoning a commonsense focus on individual agency, and thinking about the social world in terms of large collectivist forces that exist above and beyond the individuals whose actions they structure. There is a similar anti-individualistic strain even in scientifically-inclined social scientists like Durkheim and his followers as well. This is most prominent in theorists on the "structure" side of the structure-agency debate (see Ritzer 2000).

To think about how well this common anti-reductionist attitude has served the social scientists, it is very instructive to compare the anti-reductionism of the *social sciences* to anti-reductionist attitudes in the *philosophy of mind*. The question of how there could be high-level causal entities that are *not* reductively identifiable with the lower-level entities they are intertwined with has been continually refined and debated by philosophers interested in the mind-body problem for centuries. And whether most social scientists are aware of it or not, the proposals by philosophers of *mind* regarding the way in which we should think about the relationship between high and low-level entities tend to map quite nicely onto ideas about the relationship between high and low- level entities in the *social* world.[1]

---

[1] Durkheim himself thought that the relation between lower level individual facts and higher level social facts was analogous to the relation between lower level neural facts and higher level mental facts ([1898]

Now, unfortunately for the proponents of irreducible entities in the social sciences, irreducible entities have not fared so well in the philosophy of mind -- especially in the last decade. Full blown spirit/geist dualism regarding the mental has been recognizably problematic since Descartes' time. But for a long time in the twentieth century, it looked as though there was a convincing argument (based on multiple realizability) that allowed there to be irreducible high-level mental entities even in an entirely physical world. This argument, too, however, has fallen on harder times in the last decade. If the fate of irreducible high-level entities in the philosophy of mind is any guide, the status of irreducible high-level forces in the social sciences is similarly on very thin ice. In this essay I will explain why.

Mental and Social Dualism

Over the past several centuries, numerous philosophers have advocated that the mental realm, while interacting with the physical (brain) realm, was composed of a completely different kind of stuff. Some philosophers (though an ever-decreasing number) continue to do so (e.g., Foster 1991). In the social realm, social scientists have rarely been clear about exact ontological status of the social properties that they discuss (see Sawyer 2003). But if social scientists were to advocate a view analogous to the one held by these dualistic philosophers of *mind,* this view would be one of there being social forces or properties composed of a *different* sort of stuff than the activities of *people who are in* the social structures effected by these forces.

Now most social scientists, while, again, not being very explicit about the exact ontological status of social properties, tend to be reluctant to embrace a full-blown substance dualism of this sort. In the fifties, historian W.H. Dray wrote that, even social holists, while embracing some sort of irreducibility held that, "social phenomena can be said to be ontologically dependent on the actions and attitudes of individuals" (1957, 55). Nearly 40 years later, psychologist Keith Sawyer agreed, noting that "even those that reject methodological individualism (such as Giddens) nonetheless often argue that only human actors can be the sources of social action" (2003, 206). Such reluctance to fully embrace a social analogue of Cartesian dualism is clearly the expeditious course, since this sort of dualism could be seen to have had serious problems even in Descartes' time. Descartes' contemporary, Frans Burman wondered how the mind, as something completely different from the body was the sort of substance that could interact with it and guide what it does. Proponents of Cartesian dualism have never been able to satisfactorily answer this question in the philosophy of mind.[2] Social scientists who embrace some kind of social analogue of Cartesian dualism will inherit a version of this problem. As Jackson and Pettit (1992) have pointed out, if social claims are interpreted as dualistic in this way, it's unclear how high-level social forces composed of immaterial extra-individual kinds of stuff can be the sort of thing that can reach down from this separated distinct plane and *cause* the individuals existing on an altogether different plane to do anything at all.

1953). But Durkheim's exact views on the relationship between higher and lower level entities has been the subject of much scholarly debate (Alexander 1982; Lukes 1973: Sawyer 2002).

[2] Descartes himself said to Burman of this problem, "This is very difficult to explain." (But see Baker and Morris (1996) for an alternative construal of Descartes own views.)

Irreducibility and a Sparse Ontology – A Reconciliation?

But if social scientists do not want to be some kind of substance dualist about mysterious social forces moving people around (as they seem not to want to be), it's not clear in what way in the social sciences are supposed to be irreducible and autonomous. As Van Bouvel and Weber point out, "The core problem seems to be how to reconcile a form of ontological dependence of the higher-level on the lower-level with a form of explanatory independence of the higher level…" (2008, 428).

For many decades, however, it has looked as though philosophers of mind could show us a clear way that these two sorts of positions could be reconciled. Since the sixties, the dominant position on mind-body reductionism has been one called "non-reductive physicalism." Nonreductive physicalism holds that it is indeed true that nothing happens that isn't caused by particles being moved around by the forces described by physics (this is the doctrine of physicalism). At the same time, there really do exist laws about mental properties that are unable to be reductively indentified with arrangements of physical laws -- because of something called multiple realizability (hereafter, MR). It is not difficult to see how a version of the MR argument can be used to defend the irreducibility of social properties while maintaining that individuals acting is all there is to the social world.

One of the easiest ways to see how the MR argument is supposed to work is to look at an illustration first suggested by Hilary Putnam (1975): It's a law or a true generalization that a rigid square peg that is a certain length across cannot be put through a rigid round hole that is the same length across. States of affairs meeting this description can be realized by innumerable different physical systems. Yet this generalization is true whether the pegs and holes in question are huge or tiny, and it holds true no matter what the physical materials involved happen to be. It is this *multiplicity* that seems to make things problematic for physicalistic reduction. For every physical molecular account one could give detailing why in this or that set of instances, *these* pegs were prevented from passing through *these* holes, there will be other possible types of pegs and holes whose inability to pass through will have a somewhat different physical explanation. This means that no physical account of any square peg's inability to pass through a round hole will ever tell you why this is true of *every* case; no physical account will tell you why, or even that this *law* is true. There are, then, some true generalizations about certain properties that cannot be explained by physics.

Putnam used this example to argue that *mental* laws or properties were not reducible to physical ones – just as geometrical properties aren't. But Kim (2000), Ney (2008), and others have commented on how the argument is a completely general – and not restricted to the mental realm. There are apparently generalizations about frequency-dependent selection in biology, for example, that hold no matter what kinds organisms are displaying this pattern. Similarly, in the social realm, many scholars have suggested generalizations about, say, the causes and effects of revolutionary movements that, presumably, are meant to be true irrespective of any of the particular details of any particular movements. Nothing regarding the individual behavior that may explain what happens in any *particular* revolution would tell you why such generalizations hold true in all or most cases. Just as one needs a general non-reductive *geometric* account to explain what all squares can and can't do, the argument goes, multiple realizability means that one needs a general high-level *social* account in order to explain generalizations about revolutions.

The MR-irreducibility position in the philosophy of mind seems to allow one to hold that, whenever something happens, there must be physical forces acting on physical material that does the actual causing, while at the same time holding that there are generalizations about what must always happen which can't be reduced to these purely physical causings. In an exactly parallel way, someone might be what we can call an "ontological individualist" who believes that every instance of something happening in accordance with *social* laws happens only through the mechanism of some set of individuals insuring that a certain effect is produced.[3] Social laws, on this view, do what philosophers call "supervene" on laws about individuals. Only actual persons, not immaterial social laws or structures, make things happen. At the same time, these laws, being realizable in so many different ways by different arrangements of individuals, cannot be reductively identified with any kinds of dispositions of individuals. The MR argument, then, apparently gives social scientists a way of claiming that social laws and properties are autonomous from and irreducible to the properties of individuals, without having to postulate any special separate forces controlling what individuals do.

This commonly held and highly generalizable position advocated in the philosophy of mind, then, seems to be a promising way in which social scientists can defend the irreducibility of the social sciences – a view that has been long held in the social sciences, but very confusingly defended. It is interesting to note that very few social scientists, themselves, have used this strategy to defend the autonomy of the social sciences (a fact that speaks to the unfortunate isolation of these disciplines from one another.) But a number of *philosophers of* the social sciences, have, indeed pointed to an analogue of philosophy of mind's supervenience/multiple realizablity position as just the one that defenders of social autonomy ought to adopt (see, for example, Little 1991; Kincaid 1996).

Why the MR Defense Doesn't Work.

While the most promising defense of social autonomy is an analogue of the view that's been common in the philosophy mind for the past forty years, this solution is still problematic. It's important to acknowledge that over the last decade or so, there has been a growing chorus of philosophers presenting very convincing arguments that the compromise position that mental states *are* physical states but are not *reducible* to them is an unstable one (e.g., Melnyk 1995; Bechtel and Mundale 1999; Sober 1999; Jones 2004a; Kim 2000, 2005, Churchland 2005). These scholars argue that if low-level physical entities are actually all that needs to be there in making bodies behave as they do, then we can't say how the higher-level entities are doing any of the real *causing* of anything. This "causal relevance problem" has unsettled what was once a

---

[3] Note that one can be an ontological individualist about the social while being a full-blown physicalist or a serious substance dualist about the *mind*. What individual minds can or can't be explained in terms of is irrelevant to ontological individualism. What matters for ontological individualism is that the *social* realm is composed of (but not reducible to) the actions and arrangements of individual people.

widespread consensus on the irreducibility of the mental.[4]   And there is certainly no clear consensus about how to respond to it. As philosopher John Heil has pointed out, "Philosophers have offered ingenious solutions to the causal relevance problem, but none of the solutions advanced has attracted more than a handful of adherents." Because of this, he writes, for scholars committed to the irreducibility of the mental, "The mood is gloomy" (2002). If *social scientists* believed that philosophers of mind have developed arguments which can be used to demonstrate how the social sciences can be irreducible, while at the same time holding that there need not be any spooky Hegelian external entities controlling individuals, their mood should be gloomy too. Just as the arguments that appeared to *support* autonomy seemed to be general enough to justify claims of irreducibility for *both* high-level mental and high-level social properties, the newer arguments *against* irreducibility are general enough to show that we likely *don't* have autonomy in *either* domain. Over the years, a number of these anti- anti-reductionist arguments have been given, many of them quite similar to each other. Below, I'll give my own condensed version of the argument, and explain why I think both that the instability of non-reductive physicalism, in and of itself, and a parallel implausibility for anti-individualism create problems for the view that the social sciences can contain high-level irreducible properties.

The anti high-level autonomous property arguments that I've laid out in various places (2003; 2004a; 2004b) regarding the mental realm go like this: If a certain plausible physicalism is true, then whenever a *finite* disjunction of different sorts of realizers of mental state X cause a finite disjunction of different sorts of resulting behaviors or states Y, physicalism dictates that we can always just *list* all the particular conditions and physical laws that make each case of the X causing Y possible.   Many of the seemingly irreducible generalizations about mental states of the form "X's always cause Y's" can be reduced to physics in this way.[5] If there is an infinite number of X's or Y's, however, the causal closure of physics still ensures that there can't be any *non-physical* forces that ensure that only Y's result from X's.[6] And since any action can only

---

[4] Note that the causal relevance worry unsettles things irrespective of whether causes are thought of as deterministic or statistical, or whether they are thought of as more ontological or more epistemic.

[5] Putnam noticed the possibility of a disjunctive account undermining the MR argument for high-level autonomy right away, yet he did nothing to argue against it (he merely labeled it as "not a metaphysical option that can be taken seriously") (1975, 437). In "Special Sciences," Fodor tries to argue that one couldn't replace a high level law with a disjunctive list of the various lower-level circumstances and laws that realized that law, because the generalization involving that list (P_1x OR P_2x, OR....P_nx --> P_1*y OR P*$_2$ y OR......P*$_n$y, substituting for the high-level S_1x --> S_2) would not *itself be a law*. Even if Fodor were right about this generalization not being a law, it's not apparent how this really blocks the disjunctive move. If we can list every realizer of property S_1x, and say why, using lower-level laws alone, it's the case that each one of these will produce a realizer of S_2y, then why haven't we given a complete reductive explanation of why S_1x always produces S_2y? Whether it's a law or not, every case of S_1x producing S_2y is indeed accounted for, in such a scenario (see also Sober 1999).

[6] At a minimum, believing in all but the very weakest forms of physicalism requires one to assent to at least two propositions. The first is that every entity is composed of some combination of physical substances (and nothing more). The second concerns what causes these substances to do what they do. Termed "the causal closure of the physical domain," it has been described by Jaegwon Kim this way: "If you pick any physical event and trace out its causal ancestry or posterity, that will never take you outside

result from some combination of physical forces (as physicalists who believe in the causal closure of physics hold), there can't be any super/meta forces that make sure that some or other combination of contingencies and physical forces will always be on hand to guarantee that X's always result in Y's. If some combination of facts and forces always does guarantee it, then this must be because the laws of physics *alone* are such that nothing else could happen in these circumstances. Physicalism and causal closure allow there to be no mechanisms making multiply realizable generalizations true besides systematic physical forces operating on certain possible physical arrangements.

Now this argument alone, if correct, means that there can't be autonomous *social* properties that are not *reducible to physics*, in principle, if physicalism is true. But suppose, as is possible, that physicalism is untrue. Suppose there are non-physical souls. This wouldn't really help the advocate of irreducible social laws. An exactly parallel anti-autonomy argument can be made if one adopts a plausible view of social action, widely held by most social scientists– *the causal closure of individual agency*. The causal closure of individual agency holds that every event that happens in the social world is caused by no forces other than the actions of some or other set of individuals. Social anti-reductionists might want to try, like their non-reductive physicalist counterparts, to avoid the extravagant metaphysics of "social dualism" while at the same time believing that *generalizations* about what must happen can't always be reduced to these purely individualistic activities. On this view, while there are no spooky higher-level entities controlling individuals, there are, nevertheless, irreducibly social laws or properties. But the causal closure of individual agency, bars this possibility in an exactly parallel way to how the innocuous-seeming causal closure of physics causes problems for an autonomous high-level mental causes. If there are a *finite* number of individualistic psychological factors that make groups people do this or that, we can just *list* them. For example: The properties "FBI office" and "investigate" are surely multiply realizable. But that doesn't mean generalizations involving these properties must be irreducible.

Suppose an enterprising scholar used her knowledge of a) psychological principles concerning fear, suspicion, etc., b) psychological profiles of all local bureau chiefs, and c) members' general beliefs about the obligations of other members, to infer, correctly, that "Every local FBI office is currently conducting some investigation of whether one of its members is selling secrets." By doing this she has given a *reductive explanation* of why this multiply realizable generalization must be true.

And if there are an *infinite* number of ways that some or other combination of facts guarantees that a social X always makes a social Y happen, then causal closure still allows there to be *no* mechanisms to force these multiply realizable generalizations to be true aside from individualistically describable psychological factors. The social version of the causal closure principle states that *nothing* can cause anything to happen in the social world except for various arrangements of individual behavior. Since only individual behaviors ultimately cause things (according to a commonly assumed principle of causation among non-Hegelians) there can't be

_____

the physical domain. That is, no causal chain will ever cross the boundary between the physical and the non-physical" (Kim 2000, 40). The causal closure principle holds that no particle does anything without being acted upon by those physical forces typically studied in physics.

any "super" laws or forces that make sure that some or other combination of individual behaviors will be on hand to guarantee that X's always result in Y's. If some or other combination of laws always do guarantee it, then this must be because the laws and contingent facts of individual behavior *alone* mandate this. The infiniteness of the ways that they do this, doesn't mean we can't describe these ways in a finite individualistic manner. Throughout the physical sciences, we have examples of general principles of physics (along with contingent facts) that enable us to give finite explanations of certain stable behaviors in all kinds of infinitely relizable properties (e.g. pendulums) (see Batterman 2000; Jones 2004b). Such cases exist throughout the social sciences as well. The generalization that "the desire for people not to be living next to too few members of their own ethnic group will lead to highly segregated neighborhoods" is clearly a highly multiply realizable one (e.g. there's an infinite number of realizations of "neighborhood" and "segregated"). Yet Tom Schelling (1978) elegantly demonstrates how such large-scale segregation can result from the net effect of a few simple abstract principles of individual home location choice (even in situations where the abstract individuals have a preference for living in integrated neighborhoods). It doesn't matter how big or how small the multiply realized "neighborhoods" are, and it doesn't matter what sort of minority we are talking about. Here, if we have an abstract description of the dispositions of the individual units involved, we can often predict what the net effect will be in an infinite number of different situations. Examples like this can be found throughout the economic, game theory, and rational choice theory literature. If social properties really do causally explain things, on this argument, this must be because they are ultimately describable in terms of lower-level psychological dispositions. Even when social laws and properties are multiply (even infinitely) realizable, in principle, we must always be able to explain how they work in terms of individual dispositions. Social properties, therefore, can't be irreducible and autonomous.

Concluding Remarks

For the last two centuries, many social theorists have held that the social sciences are autonomous. But just why social properties could really be unable to be reduced to or explained in terms of various kinds of psychological disposition in the kinds of individuals manifesting these properties has never been clearly explicated. I've argued here that scholars who want to advocate autonomy for the social science would do well to learn from philosophers of mind, many of whom, for centuries, have tried to explicate ways in which mental properties were autonomous and irreducible to physical ones. I've claimed, however, that the lesson that they should take is that *there is no clear reason to believe there these kinds of irreducible properties really exist* – not in the mental realm and not in the social realm.

The notion of a full blown substance dualism in the mental realm has never been able to surmount the problem of how the things in one sort of realm could have any control over the things in another. The social analogue of this sort of dualism also lacks any sort of account of the mechanism by which distinct autonomous social forces could have any causal influence on individual behavior. The alternative to this sort of dualism is one in which there are no proposed distinct high-level *entities*, but there are higher-level *laws and properties* which are manifested by lower-level entities in innumerable different ways, and are thereby irreducible to lower-level dispositions. For many years, this explication of the (irreducible) relationship between mind and body has been the reigning view in the philosophy of mind. If things could really work this way in the mental realm, it is easy to see how a *parallel irreducible relationship* could exist between *social* forces and the individuals that they are intertwined with. In the last decade, however, numerous scholars have argued that, ultimately, even multiply realizable mental properties much be reducible to physical ones, if Cartesian dualism is false. As I have illustrated above, these same anti-anti-reduction arguments apply to the social realm as well. If there are no separate forces making individuals do what they do, outside of their psychological dispositions to interact with other people in things in certain ways, then even high-level multiply realizable social properties and laws, must, in principle, be re-describable in an individualistic way.

Now it must be noted, of course, that just because many seemingly convincing arguments have been given that autonomy is not an option, doesn't mean those arguments are correct. There currently exist numerous philosophers of mind who do not accept the arguments against non-reductive physicalism. There are also a few social scientists who hold that such arguments won't derail autonomy in the social realm either (see Sawyer 2003 for a good illustration). But what the existence of these anti-autonomy arguments does mean is that no one should take it as a *settled* matter that the social sciences could be autonomous. I noted earlier Van Bouvel and Weber's worry that "The core problem seems to be how to reconcile a form a ontological dependence of the higher-level on the lower-level with a form of explanatory independence of the higher level..." The fact that numerous social scholars for many years have *assumed* that the social sciences were irreducible, shouldn't obscure the fact that the question of how autonomous social laws and properties could exist has never had a clear answer. And the fact that there are now many reasons to think that even the *best* argument for autonomy is flawed continues to render the idea of irreducible social forces dubious at best. Furthermore, given that the history of science has been largely one in which seemingly inexplicable irreducible phenomena have been eventually shown to understandable in terms of a lower-level science, the burden of proof would seem to lie with the advocates of irreducibility. It's clear that they have a long way to go to meet that burden. The social realm has long been thought by many to be autonomous and irreducible from the individual one. This relationship has also long been seen to have many clear parallels with the relationship between the mind and the body. But a look at the history, especially the recent history, of the philosophical exploration of the mind-body relation indicates that the autonomy of the mental or the social is not something we should assume, or even should accept without lots more demonstration of how it could work.

References

Alexander, J. C. 1982. *Theoretical Logic in Sociology, Volume Two: The Antinomies of Classical Thought: Marx and Durkheim*. Berkeley, CA: University of California Press.

Baker, G. and K. Morris 1996. *Descartes' Dualism*. New York: Routledge.

Batterman, R. 2000. Multiple realizability and universality. *The British Journal for the Philosophy of Science* 51 (1) 115-145.

Bechtel, W., and J. Mundale. 1999. Multiple realizability revisited: Linking cognitive and neural states. *Philosophy of Science* 66 (2):175-207.

Bouwel, J. van and E. Weber. 2008. De-ontologizing the debate on social explanations: A pragmatic approach based on epistemic interests. *Human Studies* 31 (4): 423-442.

Churchland, P. 2005. Functionalism at forty: A critical retrospective. *Journal of Philosophy* 102 (1):33-50.

Dray, W. H. 1957. *Laws and Explanations in History.* Oxford: Oxford University Pres.

Durkheim, E. [1898] 1953. Individual and collective representations. Pp. 1–34 in *Sociology and Philosophy*. Glencoe, IL: Free Press. Originally published in *Revue de Metaphysique et de Morale*, 6, 1898.

Fodor, J. 1993. Special sciences. In *The Philosophy of Science*, edited by Richard Boyd, Philip Gaspar, and J. D. Trout. Cambridge, Mass.: MIT Press.

Foster, J. 1991 *The Immaterial Self*. New York: Routledge.

Hegel, G. 1977 [1807] *Phenomenology of Spirit*, trans. A. V. Miller, Oxford: Oxford University Press, 1977.

Heil, John. 2002. *Metaphysics of mind in a field guide to the Philosophy of mind* [online], [cited January 10 2002]. Available from: <http://host.uniroma3.it/progetti/kant/field/index.html>.

Jackson, F., and P Pettit. 1992: Structural Explanation in Social Theory. In *Charles, D., and K. Lennon 1992*: *Reduction, explanation and realism.* New York, NY: Oxford University Press.

Jones, T. 2003. The failure of the best arguments against social reduction and what that failure doesn't mean. *Southern Journal of Philosophy* 41 (4):547-81.

Jones, T. 2004a. Special sciences: Still a flawed argument after all these years. *Cognitive Science* 28 (3):409- 432.

Jones, T. 2004b. Reduction and anti-reduction: Rights and wrongs. *Metaphilosophy* 25 (5):614-647.

Kim, J. 2000. *Mind in a physical world.* Cambridge, MA: MIT press.

Kim, J. 2005. *Physicalism, or something near enough.* Princeton: Princeton University Press.

Kincaid, H. 1996. Philosophical foundations of the social sciences analyzing controversies in social research. Cambridge: Cambridge University Press.

Little, D. 1991. *Varieties of social explanation: An introduction to the Philosophy of Social Science.* Boulder, CO: Westview Press.

Lukes, S. 1973. *Émile Durkheim: His Life and Work*. London: Penguin Press.

Melnyk, M. 1995. Two cheers for reductionism: Or, the dim prospects for non-reductive materialism. *Philosophy of Science* 62 (3):370-388.

Ney, Alyssa. 2008. *Reductionism* [online], Internet Encyclopedia of Philosophy. [cited November 2008]. Available from: <http://www.iep.utm.edu/red-ism/>.

Putnam, H. (1975). The nature of mental states. In *Mind, language, and reality*, edited by H. Putnam. Cambridge: Cambridge University Press.

Ritzer, G. (2000). *Modern Sociological Theory*. New York: McGraw-Hill.

Sawyer, R. K. 2002. Durkheim's Dilemma: Toward a sociology of emergence. Sociological Theory 20 (2):139–283

Sawyer, R. K. 2003. Nonreductive individualism, Part II: Social causation. *Philosophy of the Social Sciences* 33 (2):203-224.

Schelling, T. 1978. *Micromotives and macrobehavior.* Cambridge, MA: Bradford.

Sober, E. 1999. The multiple realizability argument against reductionism. *Philosophy of Science* 66 (4):542-564.

Social Justice and Social Change: A Qualitative Study Examining How School Social Workers Can Aid in Decreasing Health Disparities among African American and Hispanic Adolescent Girls

Pauline Garcia-Reid
Montclair State University

Robert J. Reid
Montclair State University

Caitlin Eckert
Rutgers University

Brad Forenza
Montclair State University

David T. Lardier Jr.
Montclair State University

ABSTRACT

School social workers engage their work from an ecological lens and social justice viewpoint and, as a result, are poised to provide vital sexual health and substance abuse prevention education and services to at-risk adolescents. While most interventions often occur at the direct practice level, this need-based call highlights the macro level strategies that can be employed to increase social justice possibilities among at-risk youth. Nineteen African American and Hispanic adolescent females participated in focus group discussion to better understand the factors that are believed to contribute to substance abuse and HIV/AIDS risk among teens living in an economically at-risk community. Three emergent themes emanated from the analysis and are organized accordingly: school and community concerns, the adolescents' knowledge regarding the impact of substance abuse and HIV/AIDS in their community, and the lack of accessible prevention strategies. The findings emphasize the multiple stressors that can interfere with positive youth development and the resources and strategies that can be implemented to improve health outcomes. Recommendations for macro-level social work practice and policy are presented.

Keyword: African American and Hispanic Female Adolescents; School Social Worker; School Support; and Substance Abuse and HIV/AIDS Prevention

Introduction

Hispanic and African American girls in the United States continue to be challenged by health disparities including those associated with the dual impact of sexual risk and substance use (Center for Disease Control and Prevention (CDC), 2012; Floyd & Latimer, 2010). At some point in their lifetimes, an estimated 1 in 32 Black/African American women ages 13 and older and 1 in 106 Hispanic/Latino women will be diagnosed with HIV infection as compared to 1 in 526 white women of comparable ages (CDC[a], 2011). For minority girls residing in economically disadvantaged communities, the lack of resources to counterbalance both psychosocial and environmental threats has been associated with maladaptive coping strategies including substance use and sexual risk taking (National Institute of Drug Abuse (NIDA), 2012). For young women from low-income communities, these issues are compounded by gaps in knowledge regarding HIV/AIDS and substance abuse prevention and the lack of agents of socialization who can provide accurate and readily available health promotion information. To meet this need, school social workers are poised to assist increasing social justice possibilities and serving as advocates for change.

In the context of health disparities, social justice refers to the minimization of social and economic conditions that adversely affect the health of individuals and communities (Dilworth-Anderson, Pierre, & Hilliard, 2012). According to Levy and Sidel (2005), social justice incorporates two separate ideas grounded on the fundamental principles of justice, fairness, and equity. The first premise is that individuals should not be restricted from economic, socio-cultural, political, civil, or human rights resulting from perception of inferior status by individuals with more affluence, influence, and power. The second idea is that society must work diligently and collectively to safeguard the circumstances under which people can be healthy in terms of policies and actions that impact societal conditions. School social workers can have the greatest impact in influencing school and community environments by actively working toward these two principles.

The concept of social justice is central to the practice of social work and is a hallmark of the profession. According to the National Association of Social Workers (NASW) (2012), social justice is a core underlying guiding principle, which is rooted in equality of economic, political and social rights for all individuals. According to the NASW (2008) Code of Ethics— for example, Section 6.01— mandates a clear macro responsibility:

Social workers should promote the general welfare of society, from local to global levels, and the development of people, their communities, and their environments. Social workers should advocate for living conditions conducive to the fulfillment of basic human needs and … the realization of social justice (pp.26-27).

Macro practice is professionally guided interventions designed to bring about change in organizational, community, and policy arenas (Netting, Kettner, McMurtry, 2008). Macro activities, such as policy advocacy, community organizing, and social action, go beyond individual interventions and are often based on needs, problems, issues and concerns identified in the course of working with service recipients (Donaldson & Mayer, 2014). Since macro practice skills are necessary to confront inequalities macro practice is considered efforts intended to sustain, change, and advocate for quality of life in concert with vulnerable and underserved populations (Netting, 2005). Macro social work practice can include collaboration with consumers to strengthen and maximize opportunities for people at the organizational, community, societal, and global levels. In fact scholars have generally referred to macro practice (e.g., policy advocacy, community organizing, social action) as social work's ultimate expression of justice (Donaldson, 2007).

Using qualitative methods, the purpose of this article is twofold: 1) to examine perceived school and community concerns that are believed to contribute to negative health outcomes among African American and Hispanic adolescent females living in an economically at-risk community and 2) to assess the ways in which school social workers can engage in macro-level strategies that can aid in decreasing health disparities and serve as advocates for change. Through their training and professional commitment school social workers have the capacity to increase social justice possibilities and positively influence macro-level policies and practices impacting all students.

Methodology

Community Profile

Paterson, the third largest city in New Jersey, is located in the northeast portion of the state and is also one of the most densely populated regions in the entire country (United States Bureau, 2014). It is a racially and ethnically diverse community with a significant proportion of its residents representing Hispanic/Latino (57.6%) and African-American (46.3%) backgrounds and approximately 29% of the city's population being younger than 18 years of age (United States Census Bureau, 2014). High poverty rates also afflict the city with more than (26.6%) of its residents living below the poverty line. These environmental strains have placed this community at increased risk for many social problems including disproportionate rates of substance abuse and HIV/AIDS infection (Reid, Garcia-Reid, Forenza, Eckert, Carrier, Drag, 2014).

Study Design

Focus group methodology was utilized to examine the adolescent girls' concerns regarding school and community influences on substance abuse and HIV/AIDS risk and how school social workers can aid in offsetting negative health outcomes. Prior to initiating the interviews, IRB approval was obtained for the data collection procedures involving human subjects. Focus groups were used as the primary source of data because of the robustness of content and richness of interactions among the participants alongside the process.

Recruitment and participants

A total of three focus groups were conducted with the 19 adolescent females between the ages of 14 to 18. The first two groups consisted of six participants and the third focus group consisting of seven participants. Two-master's level researchers recruited the teens from three sites: a local high school, a program for adolescent mothers, and a school-based after school program. At the high school, the school administration and program staff informed their students about the purpose of our study, which further aided in the recruitment process. In addition, information was provided to the students during their lunch periods in their respective cafeterias and health classes. Those youth who were interested in participating in the focus group discussions informed their peers, which led to the recruitment of additional study participants.

Similar to the recruitment process that was followed at the high school, an equivalent approach at the after school program and the community-based site was adopted. These relationships were critical in helping our team gain access to our study population. By working closely with the program directors and administrators we were able to promote the study, facilitate the collection of parental consents, and secure the necessary space to conduct the focus group interviews.

The girls were told at recruitment and during the parental consent and adolescent assent process that their participation or refusal would have no bearing on their relationship with their school or participation in the afterschool or community-based programs. They were provided with food and backpack incentives upon their completion of the focus groups. However, one of the more significant problems that we encountered during the recruitment phase were delays in having parental consents signed and/or returned, which precluded several of the youth's eligibility in the focus group discussions.

The participants all indicated that they were enrolled in school at the time of the study and attended grades 9th to 12th. The racial/ethnic backgrounds of the participating adolescents consisted of Hispanic (70%) and African American (14%). Hispanics were further categorized as Dominican (37.5%), Puerto Rican (25%), undefined Hispanic/Latino (25%), and Colombian (2.5%). Some participants stated that they were biracial/bicultural being of both African American and Hispanic (16%) backgrounds. Of the sample, 47% stated that at the time of the interview they lived with only one parent/guardian. In comparison, 53% stated that they lived with more than one adult relative including at least one parent/guardian and extended relatives such as grandparents, aunts, uncles, or other adult family members. Most (87%) of the girls indicated that they were free or reduced priced school lunch recipients suggesting that their family income was at or below 185% of the poverty level.

Procedures. Focus group interviews were conducted in secluded classrooms and conference rooms. Two graduate-level female moderators, who were also members of the research staff, facilitated the focus group discussions. The facilitators had significant experience working with at-risk populations and were skilled in data collection methods. The focus group discussions lasted approximately forty-five minutes and were audio recorded with the consent of the participating adolescents. Prior to initiating the focus group conversations, participants provided basic demographic information. The discussion followed a semi-structured moderator's guide with questions presented in three domains (sensitizing concepts): environmental conditions; substance abuse and HIV/AIDS concerns; and prevention strategies and resources.

Data analysis. To organize emergent themes, an independent, doctoral-level researcher—under the direction of the principal investigators—conducted thematic analysis (Braun & Clarke, 2006) of the transcriptions. The aforementioned sensitizing concepts provided a framework through which to organize data. To bolster the rigor and confirmability of analysis, two researchers- one masters-level and one doctoral-level-coded stratified selections of the transcripts until substantive agreement (100%) was achieved, meaning that the two researchers corroborated initial interpretations and results were determined to be logically grounded in the raw data. Since confirmability is a qualitative term analogous to objectivity, having a multiple "set of eyes" to code and interpret data establishes analytical credibility. Findings, which appear below, can inform and enhance one's understandings of the constructs under study and provide logical generalizations to a theoretical examination of similar types of phenomena (Morse, 1999).

Results

Thematic Overview

Three emergent themes emanated from the analysis and are organized accordingly: 1) school and community concerns, 2) the adolescents' knowledge regarding the impact of substance abuse and HIV/AIDS in their community, and 3) prevention strategies.

School and Community Concerns.

Many youth expressed concerns regarding their broader community indicating, "*I don't like nothing*" about (this city). One female participant indicated, "*It's too violent, and I don't want to be surrounded by it.*" Another youth indicated, "*People litter and people don't care.*" Others found it difficult to identify "safe havens" in their city: "*I really don't like (this city). I don't like that it's not safe, and because it's unsafe, I can't do certain things. My mom won't let me go out when I want to go out because I have to be home at a certain time because there are people out* (who are) *crazy and stuff. It's kind of just like, Ugh.*"

The teens' concerns regarding safety emerged in several interviews and were imbedded in many more. Other girls expressed immediate threats in their school environments indicating that youth in their school "*fight every day*" and that there is a general "*lack of discipline*". Participants recognized that changing such perceptions and behaviors would have to come from individual and collective actions within the city.

Some indicated feelings of insignificance on a broader level. "*At the end of the day, it feels like nobody really cares what happens to us. It just seems like it is just how it is and how it will always be. They only pay attention when the problems reach other* (more affluent and less ethnic) *communities.* When probed more about this point, the teen indicated "*Yeah people think that Black people— you know people think that all Blacks are gonna end up in jail, dead, or on drugs and girls, yeah we're all gonna get pregnant before we graduate that is if we graduate— it's not right.*" Another teen added, "*People think because we are Black or Hispanic or because we are poor and live in* (in this city) *that we will all end up on drugs.*" And, "*They think that Hispanics will all end up a statistic because we are from here.*"

93

Substance Abuse and HIV/AIDS Concerns

Substance use was seen as a pervasive problem in the focal community and was associated with school and community conditions (Reid, et al., 2014). According to one participant, which was also emphasized by other study participants, *"You can get all kinds of drugs in* (here), *weed, cocaine, dope, crack."* The girls also indicated that drugs and alcohol were easily accessible at school too. *"You can get alcohol at school. I know people* (who) *sneak it in water bottles all the time; and weed yeah it's just as easy to get at school too,"* said another teen. *"There is violence, drugs, crime all kinds of things happening here. I think its like people sell drugs and people use drugs but its all kindda connected."* Another teen stated, *"You tell someone that you're from* (here) *and they gonna think that you're not going to become anything just because we're from* (this city). *They say, "oh that place is crazy." It's not all true though; yeah I live here but I don't do drugs; I'm not having sex; I am stronger because of where I'm from."* This later point seemed to resonate with many of the girls who seemed eager to dispel stereotypes. *"I wish there was more that we could do about all this stuff; you know— not one- on-one but overall."* Another teen added, *"I don't think we can stop every girl from using drugs or having unprotected sex but I think there needs to be more information or something out there that could maybe help girls make different choices."*

While HIV/AIDS was observed with less frequency than substance use [for example: *"You're not gonna go asking a person 'do you have HIV? Do you have AIDS? ... that's part of the problem. It's the unknown about a person."*], the youth could easily identify the risks associated with infection, saying things like: *"I don't think there's a cure for it,"* and *"you can die from it."* Similarly, some girls could identify the relationship between sexual risk taking and the contraction of HIV/AIDS *("You can get it from sexual intercourse").* Less observable was the relationship between substance use and the disease, though—when probed—girls made the association conceptualizing sexual risk as a mediator: *"When you're high and stuff like that, your perception is not as good... as if you were not on anything, and you're willing to do almost anything. You're willing to give yourself up and have sex with anybody, and not even ask them to put a condom on or if they have HIV/AIDS."*

Prevention Strategies

There was no convergence regarding the helpfulness of school-sponsored interventions. In addition, many of the girls were unable to identify any school-based action strategies aimed specially at addressing the substance abuse and HIV/AIDs prevention needs of ethnic and racial minority girls in their schools. *"I sometimes see signs in the nurses offices and stuff and that's it; but I don't really think it's making a difference."* Many of the teens also expressed that the health components were limited, too general, and did not appear to be very effective on a larger level. *"There's really nothing happening here for girls; everyone gets the same information* (males and females), *and it's really not enough; we get one marking period out of four years of high school to discuss sex education. Yeah, freshman year is the only year they talk about sex and all that. And then you get no more sex education."*

Other girls expressed their frustrations regarding their perceived lack of school-level support provided by helping professionals such as social workers. *"We are supposed to open up to them and then they make it worse because it seems like they don't really hear us; they don't really listen."*

Interestingly, the teens were outspoken about their wish to change outcomes for girls in their city. One youth indicated, *"We are more than what they* (society) *think."* Many expressed interest in becoming involved in action strategies and do their part to effectuate change. *"We don't have to follow the crowd; we can make better choices, we can lead by example"* said another youth. *"It just takes some girls speaking up and saying enough,"* added one female. *"Girls need to recognize that they have power; we need to be role models for the next generation of girls coming up"* said another female. Many of the girls, however, were unsure of how to harness their energy or impact change on a more macro-level. As expressed by one teen, *"I can work on me but I can't change what's happening* (in this city) *or* (in my school)." In general, they seemed eager to become a part of a larger action plan that could improve overall outcomes for girls in their community.

Discussion

The purpose of this study was to assess the substance abuse and HIV prevention needs of African American and Hispanic young women living in an at-risk urban environment and to examine areas for possible macro-level intervention among school social workers. Using focus group methodology, we were able to cultivate a discussion of sensitive topics – e.g., perception of school support including access to health promotion information, and the adolescents' knowledge regarding substance abuse and HIV/AIDS prevalence and risk in their community. For example, general themes emerged across interviews in which study participants were in agreement regarding environmental threats impacting their school and city, substance abuse and HIV/AIDS concerns, and the gaps in prevention strategies. Despite these obstacles, research has demonstrated that social workers are poised to promote social justice and act as social change agents on behalf of their service population (Banks, 2006).

Practice Implications

School social workers, through their academic training and professional commitment, possess the requisite skills to facilitate partnerships between groups such as parents, students, and schools and aid in cultivating health promoting school environments (Garcia-Reid, 2008). However, achieving these objectives are particularly challenging in school settings where social workers are often primarily involved in work with individual students that would, for example, facilitate adjustment, consultation, student group work, and activities related to teaming (Constable, 2009; Garcia-Reid, 2008) rather than actions associated with leadership, policy-making activities, or systems change (Bowen & Richman, 2002). While engaging in macro-level practice and policy issues may not typically be associated with school social work practice, it can provide and important often untapped avenue for potential intervention. As a first step, the CDC[b] (2011) recommends those interested in addressing health disparities should learn more about its causes and evidence-based strategies for effectively tackling specific issues among targeted groups of youth at high-risk. They should then educate school administrators, policymakers, other agencies and organizations and the public at large about these disparities and root causes, and advocate for the implementation of evidence-based, culturally-and linguistically-appropriate interventions and programs.

As a next step, school social workers must be prepared to address, on a wider level, how the intersectionality of race/ethnicity, culture, SES, and gender can influence the lived experiences of African American and Hispanic young women. For adolescent girls, this guided introspective process may allow them to begin recognizing the social, cultural, and institutional systems that may either encroach or promote their sense of self and influence their overall wellbeing. Working collaboratively to name injustices (i.e., the disproportionality of services) and identifying counteracting strategies (i.e., offering gender specific health promotion programs) may increase their sense of power and control and bring awareness to issues impacting other girls in similar circumstances. School social workers can also assist in building a sense of community among teens with the predominant goal of identifying professionally guided interventions designed to bring about planned change in schools, organizations, and communities.

Policy Implications

Schools can serve as a prime hub for bridging gender gaps in HIV/AIDS and substance use knowledge. For example, school-based social workers can fill a vital function for enabling female adolescents to be involved in conversations about sexual health and personal safety. They can also provide safe places and spaces where girls can support each other and encourage healthy behavioral choices. With the unrelenting stigma associated with female sexuality, combined with the increased risk of involvement in risky behaviors, the need for readily available sex education and health promotion programs and services are essential (Kerrigan, Andrinopoulos, Glass, & Ellen, 2008). Because many of the girls expressed concern regarding the lack of sexual health information available at their schools, examining school policies, such as one semester of sexual health education classes, would seem prudent. This study also brought to light that it is not enough to be gender neutral in service delivery, but young women are clearly in need of gender specific information that acknowledges what it means to be a racial or ethnic minority female in an economically at-risk urban setting (Small, Weinman, Buzi, & Smith, 2010). School social workers can also advocate for policies that extend and make readily available health promotion information and resources, which may offset potential environmental threats.

School social workers concerned with attending to community stressors can serve an important function in linking the family, school, and community environments. Their perspective can be invaluable in helping to shape policy initiatives. For instance, this can take the form of serving as a representative on a municipal and/or state-level coalition or task force targeting substance abuse or HIV/AIDS prevention among adolescents. Because higher levels of community strife often typify many high poverty urban environments, prevention efforts should also simultaneously examine the social and structural contexts that increase health risk among minority populations. This could also involve activities aimed at changing or influencing community conditions, standards, institutions, structures, systems, and policies (Scribner, Theall, Simonsen, Robinson, 2010). With their advocacy training and perspective, school social workers can have a hand in shaping macro-level change. School social workers can also aid in this process by strengthening and sustaining partnerships with agencies and organizations serving youth at high risk and actively involving these youth in advisory boards or youth councils that plan programs to address health disparities (CDC[b], 2011). As a final step, school social workers should, whenever possible, monitor and evaluate activities and programs targeting youth at-risk, use findings to improve programs, and document and broadly disseminate the successes, challenges, and lessons learned in reaching these teens (CDC[b], 2011).

Limitations and Directions for Future Studies

Focus group methodology was selected to answer the research question in this study for several primary reasons. First, focus groups have been utilized effectively in studies that require the discussion of sensitive topics such as sexuality, health, and drug use. Additionally, focus groups have proven effective in emphasizing discussion issues involving traditionally marginalized populations (Mitschke et al, 2008). There are, however, several limitations to this methodological approach. For example, exploration of key topics is generally limited by the size and duration of the interviews. Yet, despite these apparent limitations, we found the focus group approach to be appropriate for the exploratory nature of our investigation. Still, there remain additional unanswered questions that could serve to further contextualize the study findings. For example, parceling out the impact of segregation, discrimination, cultural adaptability, individual and family characteristics, and developmental competencies (Garcia Coll, et al., 1996) may provide deeper, more embedded explanations of the study outcomes.

Additionally, while both African American and Hispanic females participated in the study, the participation rate of African American adolescent girls was low (14%). This is particularly important because not only does the study concerns both group of girls, but also because, as previously stated, 1-32 African American women ages 13 and older will be diagnosed with HIV infection at some point in their lifetime (CDC[a], 2011). A substantial group of scholars have proposed that minorities, particularly African Americans, are distrustful of researchers because of a history of exploitation (Gamble, 1997). Others have argued that low participation rates may also be attributed to other factors such as competing priorities, lack of awareness of the problem, or the need for greater outreach among underrepresented populations (Renert, Russell-Mayhew, Arthur, 2013; Robinson & Trochim, 2007). The factors that specifically contributed to the low participation rate among African American girls in this study remain unclear. It is plausible though that some of these issues outlined above could have been at play among the teens or their parents/caregivers who may have felt apprehensive about the perceived implications of participating in the study. However, greater targeted outreach efforts could potentially increase participation rates among our focal youth. Nevertheless, despite the study limitations, there are some inferences that could be made to the broader population of African American and Hispanic girls living in at-risk communities.

There is a clear and pressing need to identify policies and strategies that extend beyond direct practice initiatives and include macro-level interventions. These efforts could serve to draw schools and communities into the fold and increase the adolescent females' ecological safety net. Supporting an expanded role of school social workers to include this wider lens could potentially lead to health promoting conversations and actions that could decrease health disparities and ultimately increase social justice possibilities among all youth living in at-risk communities.

References

Banks, S. (2006). *Ethics and Values in Social Work.* Basingstoke: Palgrave.

Bowen, G. L., & Richman, J. M. (2002). Schools in the context of communities. *Children & Schools, 24*, 67-71.

Braun V., Clarke V. (2006). Using thematic analysis in psychology. *Qualitative Research in Psychology, 3* (2), 77–101. doi:10.1191/147808876qp063oa

Center for Disease Control and Prevention (CDC)[a]. (2011). *HIV among women.* Retrieved from http://www.cdc.gov/hiv/topics/women/pdf/women.pdf.

Center for Disease Control and Prevention (CDC)[b] (2011). *Action steps to address health and educational disparities.* Retrieved from http://www.cdc.gov/healthyyouth/disparities/strategies.htm

Center for Disease Control and Prevention (CDC). (2012). Youth Risk Surveillance -United States, 2011. Morbidity and Mortality Weekly Report, 61(4). Retrieved from http://www.cc.gov/mmwr/pdf/ss/ss6104.pdf.

Constable, R. (2009). The role of the school social worker. In C.R. Massat, R. Constable, S.

McDonald, & J.P. Flynn (Eds.) *School social work practice, policy, and research* (7th ed.; pp.3-19). Chicago, IL: Lyceum Books.

Dilworth-Anderson, P., Pierre, G., Hillard, T. S. (2012). Social justice, health disparities, and culture in the are of the elderly. *The Journal of Law, Medicine & Ethics 40*(1), 26-32. DOI: 10.1111/j.1748-720X.2012.00642.x

Donaldson, L. P. (2007). Advocacy by nonprofit human services: Organizational factors as correlates to advocacy behavior. *Journal of Community Practice, 15*(3), 139-158. DOI:10.1300/J125v15n03_08

Donaldson, L. P., & Mayer, L. M. (2014). Justice as a core virtue for social work practice. *Social Work and Christianity, 41*(2), 207-231. Retrieved from http://search.proquest.com/docview/1543773416?accountid=12536

Floyd, L. J. & Latimer, W. (2010). Adolescents sexual behaviors at varying levels of substance use frequency. *Journal of Child and Adolescent Substance Abuse, 19*(1), 66-77. doi:10.1080/10678280903400701

Gamble V.N. (1997). Under the shadow of Tuskegee: African Americans and health care. *American Journal of Public Health. 87*(11), 1773–1778.

Garcia Coll, C., Crnic, K., Lamberty, G., Wasik, B. H., Jenkins, R., Garcia, H., & McAdoo, H. P. (1996). An integrative model for the study of developmental competencies in minority children. *Child Development, 67*, 1891-1914.

Garcia-Reid, P. (2008). Understanding the effect of structural violence on the educational identities of Hispanic adolescents: A call for social justice. *Children & Schools, 30*(4), 235-241. doi:

10.1093/cs/30.4.235

Kerrigan, D., Andrinopoulos, K., Chung, S., Glass, B., & Ellen, J. (2008). Gender ideologies, socioeconomic opportunities, and HIV/STI-related vulnerability among female, African-American adolescents. *Journal of Urban Health, 85*(5), 717-26. doi:10.1007/s11524-008-9292-9

Levy, B. S. & Sidel, V. W. (2005) The nature of social injustice and its impact on public health In B.S. Levy & V.W. Sidel (Eds.) *Social injustice and public health* (pp. 3-20), New York, NY: Oxford University Press. DOI:10.1093/acprof:oso/9780195171853.001.0001

Mitschke, D.B., Matsunaga, D.S., Loebl, K., & Tatafu E. (2008). Multi-ethnic adolescents' attitudes toward smoking: A focus group analysis. *The Science of Health   Promotion, 22*(6), 393-398. doi:10.4278/ajhp.22.6.393

Morse, J. M. (1999). Qualitative generalizability. *Qualitative Health Research, 9*(1), 5-6. Retrieved from http://search.proquest.com/docview/220268513?accountid=12536

National Association of Social Workers. (2008). *Code of ethics of the National Association of Social Workers.* Washington, DC: Author

National Association of School Social Workers (NASW). (2012). NASW Standards for School Social Workers Services. Retrieved from http://www.naswdc.org/practice/standards/naswschoolsocialworkstandards.pdf.

National Institute of Drug Abuse (NIDA). (2012). Drug Abuse and HIV. Retrieved from http://www.drugabuse.gov/sites/default/files/rrhiv.pdf.

Netting, F. E. (2005). The future of macro social work practice. *Advances in Social Work 6*(1), 51-59.

Netting, F., Kettner, P., & McMurtry, S. (2008). Social work macro practice (4th ed.). Boston, MA: Allyn and Bacon.

Reid, R. J., Garcia-Reid, P., Forenza, B., Eckert, C., Carrier, M., & Drag, S. (2014). Let Our Voices Be Heard: Urban Minority Adolescents Share Their Perspectives Regarding Substance Abuse and HIV/AIDS Prevention Messages. *American Journal of Health Promotion.* doi: http://dx.doi.org/10.4278/ajhp.130117-QUAL-34

Renart, H., Russell-Mayhew, S., & Arthur, N. (2013). Recruiting ethnically diverse participants into qualitative health research: Lessons learned. *The Qualitative Report, 18*(23), 1-13. Retrieved from http://www.nova.edu/ssss/QR/QR18/renert23.pdf

Robinson, J.M. & Trochim, W. M. K. (2007). An examination of community member's researchers' and health professionals' perceptions of barriers to minority participation in medical research: An application of concept mapping. Ethnicity & Health, 12(5), 521-539. doi:10.1080/13557850701616987

Scribner, R., Theall, K.P., Simonsen, N., Robinson, W. (2010). HIV risk and the alcohol environment: Advancing and ecological epidemiology for HIV/AIDS. *Alcohol Research & Health, 33* (3), 179-183.

Small, E., Maxine, L. W., Ruth, S. B., & Peggy, B. S. (2010). Explaining condom use disparity among black and hispanic female adolescents. *Child & Adolescent Social Work Journal, 27*(5), 365-376. doi:10.1007/s10560-010-0207-8

United States Census Bureau. Paterson, NJ. Available at: http://quickfacts.census.gov/qfd/states/34/3457000.html. Accessed October 7, 2014.

Acknowledgement: This research was supported by Grant No. SP-15104 from the Substance Abuse and Mental Health Services Administration (SAMHSA), Center for Substance Abuse Prevention (CSAP). The findings and conclusions in this article are those of the authors and do not necessarily represent the views of the Substance Abuse and Mental Health Services Administration (SAMHSA), Center for Substance Abuse Prevention (CSAP).

About the Authors

Pauline Garcia-Reid, PhD, is an Associate Professor in the Department of Family and Child Studies with an affiliate appointment in the Robert D. McCormick Center for Child Advocacy and Policy at Montclair State University. Her research interest include youth substance use & violence prevention, social justice and advocacy within a culturally-grounded social work lens, and practice and research with racial and ethnic minority children and families.

Robert J. Reid, is a Professor in the Department of Family and Child Studies at Montclair State University. His research interests include community based participatory research, substance abuse and HIV/AIDS prevention among urban minority youth structural and environmental interventions to reduce risk factors and to promote protective factors associated with various health behaviors, such as adolescent substance abuse, sexual risk, and youth violence.

Caitlin Eckert, MSW, is a PhD. student at Rutgers University School of Social Work. Her research interests include sex education, at-risk youth, and power-based violence.

Brad Forenza, Ph.D., is an Assistant Professor in the McCormick Center for Child Advocacy and Policy at Montclair State University. There, his research foci include youth development, civil society, and social policy.

David T. Lardier Jr., M.Ed., LAC, is a doctoral student and Fellow in the Family Studies PhD program at Montclair State University. Mr. Lardier's research interests focus on understanding socio-cultural and environmental factors that affect urban-minority youth and the empowerment-based mechanisms present that mitigate negative behaviors.